Angel Parent Memories

THIS TREASURY OF HEARTWARMING STORIES

IS A CELEBRATION OF LIFE

SO NO CHILD WILL EVER BE FORGOTTEN

Carmen D'Amico

ANGEL PARENT MEMORIES
FLORIDA

May angels wrap you in their love and protect your journey —
Carmen D'Amico

Published by ANGEL PARENT CO, INC.
PO Box 11346
Ft. Lauderdale, FL 33339-11346
954.772.4111
www.angelparent.com

This book was set in Adobe Caslon
Cover Design and Composition: Jonathan Pennell
Cover Illustration: Timothy Leistener, Ft. Lauderdale, Florida

Library of Congress Catalog Number: Applied For
D'Amico, Carmen
Angel Parent Memories
ISBN: 0-9747512-0-0

First Edition
10 9 8 7 6 5 4 3 2 1
Printed in the United States of America

Dedication

* * * *

For my son, Paul

Who was the inspiration

For ANGEL PARENT

Acknowledgements

* * * *

EVERY AUTHOR, NOVICE OR SEASONED, owes much to everyone who helps them put their manuscript together. Fifty or more people may be responsible for the monumental tasks that strive for perfection in order for a book to be enjoyed and appreciated.

This book is different. Millions of parents have lost sons or daughters and suffered so much pain. It was time we had a title to call ourselves. Now we are respectfully named ANGEL PARENTS.

It has taken centuries for the phrase ANGEL PARENT to come to us and today we have a book of memories to share which are the stories we've carried in our hearts.

Most of these stories were written in tears, a few written in blood, all were written with much love. Read them and remember you are being entertained by a cast of angels.

Everyone who shared a story has given you a little piece of their heart. They have opened old wounds so you could know something about their special angel. These were the children you heard laughing in playgrounds or on the beach. Others were heroes who shed their blood and died for you. Many were the nice kids who carried your groceries to your car or gave you a seat on the bus. You have met them before and you will meet them again in the pages of this book.

If you or someone you know is an ANGEL PARENT, your story should follow in the next edition so that your child will be remembered in the same sweet, honorable manner.

Relive the beautiful journeys they had, the risks they took, the love they shared and lost.

Thank you, ANGEL PARENTS, and know that you are recognized with the highest esteem by our Almighty Creator. Because of our ANGELS, this book is for you.

—***Carmen D'Amico***

Contents

* * * *

SECTION IV: LOYALTY

SECTION V: TICKLING THE FUNNY BONE

SECTION VI: THE INNOCENCE OF CHILDREN

SECTION VII: TEACHING AND LEARNING

SECTION VIII: RANDOM ACTS OF KINDNESS

SECTION IX: ACHIEVING THE DREAM

Foreword

* * * *

HEALING IS THE WORD that comes to mind when you read *Angel Parent Memories*. Carmen D'Amico has provided the world with a treasury of 50 heartwarming stories that foster the natural healing of the emotional body.

At last the parents who suffer from the loss of a beloved child can participate in a project that allows them to preserve and share precious memories of their children. These memories unite them in a common bond with other Angel Parents who are handling the grieving process in a positive manner.

Acceptance and recovery come in stages in the grieving process. Each of us has our own way of dealing with tragic circumstances that occur in our lives. *Angel Parent Memories* is a venue that paves a golden street to recovery by allowing a celebration of the child's life.

Within this book you will discover diamonds, pearls and precious jewels. In each story you are awakened to the reality that everyone is born special. Each child has his or her own uniqueness that can never be duplicated. Spirituality, learning lessons, acts of courage, random acts of kindness, and even humorous events express the life experiences of these children and serve as highlights in the parents' heart felt memories. Each story lends a sense of permanence and individuality to the child's previous existence.

Showing appreciation of these loved and cherished children is the reason for this book. The book is a way of sharing mutual feelings of grief. It is a way of reaching out to lessen the burden of loss that the parents have claimed for their own. By sharing their stories with others they are able to see a continuation and recognition of their child's life.

Parents from all walks of life share touching, heartwarming, and memorable moments in the lives of their Angel Children. Seeing the child through the eyes of the parent allows us to find answers in our own quest to understand the variables in life.

After reading this book you will be left with a warm, fuzzy feeling and a whole lot of tender wisdom tucked away in your heart. You will walk away a better person with a greater appreciation for life. You will leave with the inspiration to totally appreciate your own children while you have them.Now you are able to see the silver threads that connect your heart to that of your child. I am reminded of a beautiful garden that is filled with flowers that beckon you to lean over to smell their nectar. Amidst all the splendor and wondrous flowers sits the Master tending the garden. As God's love radiates throughout the garden it rests upon the young plants. I can clearly see the silver threads as He spins a wondrous web of love and protection. These silver threads run through this book from the beginning to the end. This is indeed the earmark of a continuing blessing as Carmen D'Amico embarks on the first of her series of *Angel Parent Memories.*

— R. Winn Henderson, M.D.
#1 Nationally Best Selling Author and
Host of the Internationally Syndicated Radio Talk Show:
Share Your Mission.
www.theultimatesecrettohappiness.com

SECTION ONE

* * * *

Acts of Courage

SEE IT MY WAY

JACK

FOR AS LONG as I could remember, Jack was constantly telling his kid brother, Adam, to try to see things his way. Simply because he was nineteen months older, Jack felt he could guide Adam. You see, Jack was logical, organized, pensive, determined. Adam was spontaneous, scattered, carefree and high spirited. They respected and loved each other as brothers but at times their disagreements drove me up the walls.

Jack had more going for him culturally whereas Adam felt when he was ready, he'd catch up in a few giant strides. They were young; time was on their side.

Jack liked girls who were studious, serious about life, conservatively dressed brunettes with neat hair. He felt they were more grounded, would make better life partners.

Adam liked blondes with long hair who liked to have fun, disco, drink beer and skinny dip. Adam wasn't interested in a life partner, at least not today. Maybe tomorrow.

"Adam, don't you think it's time you settled down with just one girl and stop playing the field? One day somebody's going to break your fickle heart and it won't be pretty. For once, why don't you try to see things my way?" spoke Jack in his big-brother tone of voice.

Adam said making a commitment at this stage of his life would be like throwing away his candy jar.

He liked the competition of two or three girls who vied for his attention.

Whenever they had a silly dispute, Jack would try to set examples for Adam to think things through. Adam's perceptions of this meant working inside certain restrictions.

He'd repeat, "Adam, just this once, try to see things my way." Adam rarely did.

Life plays tricks on us sometime when our back is turned. Both boys wound up in the Army because of their Army Reserve status. It was an especially difficult time for me to know both my sons were being shipped overseas. The only good part, if any, was that they were together. It was very little comfort and I tried to hide my feelings from their father, but what's a mother to do?

At the earlier stages of the Iraq war Jack and Adam were flown to Quwait for training in the ambience of the desert. The country was a dust bowl. During the day the temperature could easily reach a whopping 135 degrees. The blistering sun fried everything to a crisp. Energy was easily depleted. Tempers flared along with the blinding light of day.

This was not a primitive style war fashioned out of foxholes, bayonets and grenades. Here was a streamlined, computerized fighting machine which centered on lasers, pyrotechnics and every fancy name in the world of hi-tech performance. The only thing modern-day science failed to discover and manufacture was a layer of impenetrable skin to protect our men.

If you cut one, he still bled.

Americans tuned in 24/7 to watch an in-your-face, up-close-and-personal war from their cushy Lazy-Boys. In spite of myself I sat watching most afternoons with my dog at my feet while I munched on crumpets and tea and for all intents and purposes, I kept reminding myself that this was, and is, WAR!

Within a period of several days, the troops were making their way northward to Baghdad where the thickest measure of fighting was taking place. Each man was bundled with a pair of heavy combat boots, helmet, high-powered weapon and a backpack that was heavy enough to set up a camp.

Behind them were Abrams tanks with nearly as many gizmos on the dashboard as you'd find in an airplane cockpit. Rolling nearby a parade of trucks carrying every kind of artillery firing machine gun, ammunition, and emergency medical supplies. Sergeants in the fields carried laptops, cell phones, digital watches and green goggles for detecting the enemy's location in pitch-black darkness. This was no Boy Scout summer camp in the Pocono Mountains.

Without much ado the orders came through that in two days they were going to attack from their vantage point. The men, some of which looked like fifteen-year-old boys who were just starting to shave their peach-fuzz cheeks, were told to get some sleep as the next day was going to be bedlam.

Who could sleep under such stress? Very soon these strangers would become as close as kin.

The day dawned early and the sun was like a relentless dragon breathing his fiery breath on everything in his path. Like molten lava it scorched the earth and parched the skin.

With little more than a three-two-one signal, all Hell broke loose. Guys came running out of hiding, artillery shells phhht'd across the barrenness, everyone was screaming orders. Once raised to be the boys-next-door, these people were now trained to discharge weapons of war.

The air was filled with dust, smoke and a gray rain of artillery which looked like sleet in the light of day. Shells from the Abrams tanks boomed a declaration they would crush everything in their path.

The Iraqi soldiers put up a strong fight but their makeshift outposts went down like a house of cards.

By high noon the air was polluted with all the debris of telltale warfare. The dust smoke screen was so dense, it made targeting almost impossible. On both sides men were dropping like flies from heat exhaustion; casualties escalated. Planes like giant dragonflies zeroed in on the enemy dropping bombs like a drenching summer rain. There was so much yelling going on, it was quite-near impossible to discern which side it came from.

A sudden hail of artillery trained on Adam's position landed almost at his feet. The exploding shrapnel caught Adam's face like a giant monster claw ripping off his nose, ear and spurting blood from his eyes. The impact threw him backward landing him with a dull thud as his body turned red instantly.

Without hearing another order or shot, Jack leapt to Adam's side. He picked him up and, throwing him over his shoulders, Jack sped toward the convoy of trucks in a line-up.

"Hold on, Adam. I gotcha now. Don't worry, bro. I'm gonna get you out of this hellhole. Just hold tight, hear me? Stay with me, Adam, just another...." At that moment an Iraqi's bullet got lucky catching Jack through the heart. Both guys went sprawling as they hit the dirt.

A hovering chopper picked them up and flew them to a nearby makeshift hospital where teams of tireless doctors, nurses and Red Cross were working feverishly on as many wounded as arrived minute by minute. Haggered by the sleepless shifts and stench of blood and guts, everyone drew on their inner reserves of energy to tend to the men who were crying out in unfathomable pain from bodies blown open and limbs torn away.

On opposite tables lay Jack and Adam, immediately hooked up to blood transfusions, IVs and megadoses of antibiotics. Jack was looked at, labeled "flatliner" and he was taken away. His heart had been shredded and the hole was so huge, you could have put a fist through the place that held his heart.

Adam's entire head was swathed in bandages. A tiny slit let in his trach tube, two hoses inserted into little holes that once were his nose. Three bulbous packings represented his shot-off ear and splattered eye sockets. God bless them; they never knew what hit them.

Nearly three weeks later Adam roused from his coma just long enough to hear his commander tell him that while he was not a candidate to model for *GQ magazine*, he had a chance to recover. Yes, he'd need several plastic surgical procedures to restore his face. They explained they could build a new nose with cartilage taken from elsewhere in his body and restore his features with fat from his behind.

Adam couldn't speak yet. Gesturing as if to write, the doctor handed him a pen and paper. He wrote Jack's name with a question mark. The doctor explained that Jack took a bullet in an attempt to save Adam's life. The news was too much. Adam wanted to cry but he had no tear ducts. He cried with all the tears his heart could hold. The orderly pushed a sedative into his IV to help stop the convulsive shakes his body made as he groaned with overwhelming sorrow for his beloved Jack. Then he surrendered to sleep.

Several weeks went by. Surgeries went by. Sadness went by and came back and went by again.

The specialists gathered around Adam in the darkened room. Adam was sitting in a wheelchair clenching his fists. His palms were clammy and beads of sweat trickled down his chest. His feet were ice cold in his heavy athletic socks. His back hurt from the tension and he heard a slight wheeze as he drew in a breath.

Breathing through his new nose was a very strange sensation. He didn't know when his nose was running as he didn't have any sensation yet. Would it itch like a real nose, he wondered? Would his sniffer detect Mom's Thanksgiving turkey in the oven or the warm apple pie on the holiday table? Would he ever be able to smell a woman's perfume behind her ears, he questioned himself.

Snip. Snip. Snip. The surgeon was delicately cutting away the bandages around his head. Removing them would be like going out in the snow without a ski cap, he mused.

"Hold still now, buddy. Just a few more cuts and you'll be free. Don't open your eyes until I ask you to. The optic nerves are extremely sensitive and need time to adjust."

Here came the big breakthrough. "Adam, we didn't want to tell you sooner because we didn't know whether or not we'd be successful. We've transplanted Jack's corneas in an effort to restore your sight."

Adam was breathless, stunned. He wanted to cry but it wouldn't come.

There was a slight glimmer of light now. More bandages came off.

Drops were inserted under the bandages to saturate and moisturize the eye sockets.

"Ok, Adam. On the count of three, open your eyes verrrrry slowly. The nerves need to adjust.

Here we go. Now, onnnnnnne, open slightly. Good. Twoooooo, give me a little more. Good. Threeeee.

Look straight at me, Adam." The surgeon looked into Adam's eyes with a tiny light. He sighed and nodded.

Adam stared long and hard into the mirror someone handed him and saw Jack's hazel eyes in his sockets. He was hypnotized with the awesome realization that he and Jack's eyes would see the world.

Adam garbled in a very hoarse voice still rasping from injured vocal chords,

"Thanks, Jack. I love you so much, bro. From now on I'll see everything....your way!"

* * * *

Melanie (name withheld by request) is a grandmother to Adam's little girl, Jackie, named in honor of her Uncle Jack. Adam is happily married to a brunette with short hair. It's become an inside family joke.

ANGELS HAVE MEDALS, TOO

JASON WHITAKER

SOME PEOPLE WERE JUST BORN to be heroes while most of us usually are too frightened to act. At this time of my life I no longer question the "whys" and "wherefores."

My plans did not include going north that summer but when my sister Vera called to say her husband had some health problems, I felt I couldn't turn her down.

Vera never learned to drive a car in spite of everyone's insistence and now, her vision wouldn't permit anyhow. Going up there meant she had work to be done around the property and living on a fixed income, my family usually pitched in to see them through the rough times.

Jason was seventeen at the time and all that intensive weight training was paying off. His body was rippled with hard muscle and he found every excuse to use his brawn.

He swam and ran five miles nearly everyday to keep up. A nice pair of abs and a great set of buns in tight jeans never hurt in the female department and it certainly didn't do much to crimp his style. I could imagine what he'd look like when he reached twenty-three.

We settled in quickly at Vera's house and her husband, Bernie, kept moving about trying to look like he was in the best of health as if not to worry us much more. But I could tell he was putting on an act by trying to masquerade his pain now and then.

They were early risers and by the time I came into the kitchen for coffee, Vera was already baking brownies or stuffing a chicken for dinner. Her kitchen always had that wonderful aroma that seems to surround good cooks.

The first few days were wonderful. Vera and I would drive to the mall and catch up on family gossip and the men would be doing little jobs that must have been waiting all winter gathering dust. It felt like a family reunion, soft and comfy as an old pair of shoes.

Looking out the screen door I caught glints of sunlight forcing their way through the tall branches of the oak trees that shaded the back yard. It was such a peaceful place.

There were all types of wildflowers and a Rose of Sharon bush the bees loved as much as I.

For me it might have been ideal but with those trains passing all through the night...

The trains ran past their house in a deep ravine at the end of their property which was protected by a high cyclone fence. Well, what did it matter in the grand scheme of things? I didn't have to live there and, if it was good enough for Vera, it was good enough for me.

Vera told me about the seriousness of Bernie's condition. He was having kidney failure which meant he needed dialysis treatments. Not knowing much about it at that time, it seemed like a monumental challenge; but, the local kidney center had a van to pick up the patients which was a relief for Vera and me.

That Thursday morning I was awakened by the train whistle. I hadn't heard it in a long time and it brought back some fun memories of my childhood in that town. I guess one could get used to it if one had to.

When I got to the kitchen, the fragrant smell of homemade soup filled my nostrils.

Vera had a vegetable garden which she took great pride in and her New Jersey tomatoes were prize worthy. Just then she came in from the root cellar with her arms full of preserves, some spices and a few of the largest, reddest tomatoes I'd ever seen.

She was rinsing them at the sink when we heard a crack like the sound of lightning. Bernie let out a scream from the yard which sounded like someone was being murdered. Vera began screaming as she stood frozen in fear at the window.

I ran straight for the screen door and onto the back porch. Bernie was holding onto the fence with one hand, howling. His body was shaking convulsively and jerking back and forth. At once I knew exactly what had happened. The recent storm must have knocked down a railway wire which ran parallel to the fence. It landed on the fence and unknown to Bernie, the wire was as live and murderous as a sniper with a bayonet.

I ran toward him yelling, "Jason! Jason!" Jason was already coming from behind the root cellar door and racing toward Bernie. Meanwhile Bernie was being electrocuted before our eyes and I knew Vera was witnessing this entire scenario from her window view.

"Don't touch him! Don't touch him!" I yelled to Jason who was quickly approaching Bernie. Bernie's face was screwed up in the most painful grimace. He was unable to disengage himself from the fence as thousands of volts of electricity passed through him.

The cable looked like a hundred foot snake dancing wildly before our eyes, whipping Bernie's body up and down. It was as if he were hypnotized while bright blue and white flashes sparked from the cable and went coursing through his body.

Vera ran back to the house to dial 911. In the background I could hear her sobbing and trying to give her address to the operator. I wondered how long it might take for a fire rescue truck to get here and if so, would Bernie still be alive by then?

Jason had jumped up to catch a huge limb from a nearby tree and swinging up and down from it, the limb snapped dropping itself and Jason to the ground. He grabbed the giant limb and, using it like a lance, he moved in toward the menacing cable.

The cable thrashed against the fence. Somehow it was caught onto the fence and couldn't break free. It was as if it were a living, breathing monster. Whenever Jason tried to push it aside, it spat out more sparks. It was as if it knew Jason was there and it reacted more violently. It was like the Devil himself were in our midst. The thought of it made me shudder.

Jason kept trying but nothing was working. He was frantically poking at the electrical snake to dislodge it from the fence. It was too heavy and

Jason had no luck. Quickly and deftly he pushed against Bernie's body so hard with the limb, the electrical current sent Bernie sprawling five feet from the fence but at last, he was freed.

Bernie lay on the ground, his upper torso fried, his flesh turned black as scorch.

The moment Bernie's grip from the fence was severed, the evil black snake came to rest on the fence, content with the job it had done to show us its unforgiving strength.

I could see little puffs of smoke emanating from Bernie's shirt and I was too scared to get near him. Grabbing a watering can nearby, I doused him and almost waited for the usual hissing sound like a fry pan being splashed with tap water. There was no sound.

Vera came running, crying and cursing because she had no clue as to why God brought this terrible end to her beloved Bernie. She said, "He didn't deserve to die like this." When she uttered those words, I looked immediately at Bernie's chest, and to my surprise, he was still breathing. There was a good God, after all, I assured myself.

Jason had pulled a summer blanket from the porch swing and covered Bernie's trembling torso. I patted his face with watered hands as if to cool his skin. I felt very stupid somehow. Why didn't I know more about these things, I asked myself? Hadn't I raised a child? Why didn't I have more knowledge for an incident such as this?

The fire rescue team and an ambulance team both arrived simultaneously. The paramedics went to work instantly on Bernie while a police officer took notes from Jason.

Some others administered oxygen, IV's were pushed into Bernie's arms, people were checking his vital signs, making remarks, preparing a stretcher. It was like a three-ring circus. Ten minutes ago you wouldn't have known there were people within a five-mile radius and now, about fifteen men and women were working in all directions to stabilize Bernie before attempting to get him to a hospital. I was witnessing class-A teamwork.

At first it looked like a lot of confusion but, when you listened closely, it all made sense. Every person was doing something specialized to create a team-effort life-saving act.

Meanwhile someone was patting Jason on the back for thinking on his feet. If he had not been quick enough to pull Bernie's body from the fence, he would have received too much voltage and he wouldn't have made it this far. I managed a silent prayer and wondered if his condition would not allow him to pull through this traumatic experience. I wondered how many points it would take to be in God's favor to know whether or not one gets to go on living. It remained to be seen.

Jason was just a little behind the rescue team, crouched on the ground crying. The realization of what happened finally hit him and he had broken down in tears and despair.

A policewoman was comforting Vera as she tried to get closer to Bernie but she wasn't able to pull herself together. I brought her over to a tree bench and we sat down. With our arms around each other, we cried for Bernie and ourselves. He was all she had.

At the hospital we waited for hours while Bernie underwent extensive surgical procedures to save his life. Vera was emotionally drained, asleep now with her head on a pillow. My eyes smarted from crying and I knew our trip up here would extend itself into a month or more. Jason was nervously pacing the floor so I sent him to the cafeteria to pick up something to eat as we hadn't had a thing to nourish us in several hours. He returned with several things but no one felt like eating anyhow. I drank all three coffees.

Oh, why wouldn't someone come out and tell us something? I wondered if Bernie would be able to resume any quality of life after this, if he survived at all. Of course, I didn't want to express my fears to Vera but I'm sure the same thoughts nagged at her, too.

It was past 7 p.m. when the doctor came out to tell us Bernie had pulled through but it was going to be a long, tedious recovery. He would require tons of therapy and some time in a rehabilitation center for burn victims.

Nobody slept much that night. The phone didn't ring so I repeatedly told Vera that "no news was good news." I slept in her bed to keep her company and she cried every time she woke up and realized Bernie wasn't there. It was the longest night of her life, I'm sure.

Jason brought in the morning paper and tossed it on the kitchen table. I wasn't in the mood for headlines so I never even glanced at it. Vera was having coffee, repeating the events of yesterday over and over and by 10 o'clock I was about ready to scream.

Poor girl, I couldn't blame her. She looked like a ghost, pale and showing huge dark circles under her eyes. When the phone finally rang, it was the nurses' station giving us an update on Bernie's condition. He was stabilized but not yet conscious.

Vera asked if I had seen the paper. She said the nurse told her there was a story about Bernie and Jason. I ripped open the Local section and there was a blaring headline...

"Young Hero Risks Life To Save Uncle." Quickly I scanned the article and with tears brimming in my eyes, I thanked God, Jason and whoever else was responsible for what good took place. I was happy that we were there to help at such an important time.

The article praised Jason's quick thinking and dexterity to handle the situation which nearly killed his uncle. It went on to mention how, given a little more time, Bernie would not have been so lucky. Jason, my son, a hero. It might not have sounded like an act of bravery, but his persistence and strength are what it was all about.

Five weeks later we pulled into our driveway, exhausted from a summer of overkill.

The work we had faced was a calling for Jason and me to be where we were needed most. When we opened the door to the living-room, a shout went up.

"SURPRISE!" Our nearby friends and neighbors had prepared a "Hero Welcome Party" for Jason and our Mayor was there to award Jason with a medal for meritorious service in the face of danger. Through his modest veneer I could see he was happy and proud for the recognition being given him.

Today I look back at my son's bravery and say "thank you, God" for his chance to play the hero in his brief lifetime. Surely he must an angel with a halo...and a medal.

* * * *

Marian Karikov lives in a retirement community in Georgia, with her sister, Vera. Her hobbies are reading and tending her plants. She and Vera still go to the mall and buy 1000-piece puzzles which they work on together. When they are completed, Marian glues them together, frames them and sells them at their local charity bazaars.

COKE BOTTLE GLASSES

CORRINNE HAMILTON

"I HATE THEM! I HATE THEM!" Corrinne came running into the entryway, slamming the front door and throwing her school books on the floor. She ran directly upstairs to her room and slammed another door.

No one had to tell me what was wrong. I could venture a pretty accurate guess.

The kids at school were making fun of her "coke bottle glasses" again. They'd call her "four eyes" and "blind-as-a-bat" and the usual cruel things kids say to hurt the underdog.

Like many other days she was crying when I entered her little bedroom. It was nearly futile to try to make her feel better. As long as she had those glasses, nothing was going to help. Her Dad and I tried a hundred times before and we always came up empty.

Moving to another house, street or city wasn't the answer. It would always be like this until she was old enough to stand up for herself. Meanwhile, there was this unbearable burden she had to live with and my heart broke for her.

Corrinne was a smart, polite child with potential to make something of herself given the opportunity. Apparently, the outside world wasn't about to give her any breaks.

She was going to have to steel herself for a lot of hard knocks and it wasn't going to be easy.

We spoke with specialists who informed us that Corrinne had a particularly rare eye disease. She was too young to have the surgery needed to replace certain deficiencies before she would be able to have any success with her vision. Technologies were improving but not nearly as quickly as we had hoped. Many years later, lasers and state-of-the-art methods would be put into place but, at that time in her life, Corrinne had little hope.

Taking her in my arms and rocking her, I smoothed her hair and said, "Don't worry, honey. One of these days you'll grow into a brilliant young lady who will outsmart all those nasty kids. You'll be able to prove to everyone that glasses didn't hinder you."

Lord, that sounded so lame, I could have kicked myself. And well I should have.

I tried to do everything I could to help Corrinne overcome her problem. Her Dad and I wanted her to be special for her sake so she could be head and shoulders above the crowd who made her life miserable.

We gave her piano lessons, ballet and tap classes, whatever made her happy.

She studied hard and she made very good grades despite her heavily scheduled classes.

I made sure she had nice clothes and taught her very good manners so she would never have to feel out of place in any social situation. Other parents admired her courage but at PTA I often caught the tsk tsk remarks behind our backs. I had to live with it.

One day Corrinne didn't get home from school at her regular time. I thought she may have missed the bus but no, that wasn't like her. She was usually right in line. When it got past 4 o'clock, I began to feel nervous. I called some other children's parents to ask if they'd seen Corrinne. From those who answered my call, no one had seen my daughter and all of a sudden, fear took over. I jumped into my car and raced to the school.

The schoolyard was empty, doors locked, only the janitor was cleaning up and he didn't remember seeing any eight-year-old in the vicinity. I stopped the first police car and told him I was searching for Corrinne. He put out a BOLO alert and I followed him to the police station to fill out a report. They called my husband and he had his office workers call local hospitals and the city morgue. He came down to the station and we waited to hear if anyone reported seeing our daughter. Silently we began to think the worst.

I tried not to think bad thoughts but it's almost like a knee-jerk reaction. Now and then I'd look into Larry's face and it was written there as plain as I could decipher it.

We imagined what might have happened to Corrinne. A thousand questions came up and the least frightening possibility was that Corrinne had been kidnapped. Unless she was held against her will, Corrinne wasn't the type to wander off with a stranger.

At around 6 o'clock the Police Chief told us to go home; he'd call us at once if they got any news. How empty that sounded. Did he think for a minute we could just go home as if nothing happened? Did he think we were so heartless and impersonal? What did we look like, a couple of jerks who could easily go home, cook a steak and eat it as though nothing different were taking place? I became so incensed, I began to argue. Larry stepped in immediately to calm me; he said there was nothing they could do at the moment.

Reluctantly, we went home in our cars but, before we got into the house, I jumped in Larry's car and said, "Let's go to the school and ask if we can look inside Corrinne's desk." I thought perhaps there might be a clue as to her whereabouts.

Fortunately, the janitor was still on the premises and Larry told him why we needed to see Corrinne's desk. Against all rules, he sensed our agitation and he let us in.

Her desk appeared as though nothing had been disturbed. I kind of hoped I'd find something out of line so perhaps we'd have a clue as to what might have transpired.

On the way home I recounted the things I'd seen in Corrinne's desk. Something wasn't quite right. I urged Larry to return to the police station. He didn't hesitate. Larry knew me well enough to know that if I had a hunch about something, we'd best play it.

I asked to see the Police report. There was nothing in it that was out of the ordinary.

Looking through Corrinne's desk I thought I saw an eyeglass case. Corrinne took off her glasses only for gym class. Her last class was gym that day. That meant she was at the gym but her glass case was empty. Apparently she never got to the gym and she was probably still wearing her glasses and the glass case laid in the desk untouched. Or, did she ever make it to the gym at all?

Larry telephoned the principal at his home, apologizing for the disturbance. He explained what I had seen and the principal said he'd look into it in the morning. We got in touch with the police and they went to the school, gained entrance and removed all the items from Corrinne's desk. All but one. The eyeglass case was missing.

My blood ran cold when I heard that revelation. Now we were certain something awful happened to Corrinne. This was going to be a long day's journey into night.

Larry and I stayed up most of the night going over all the facts with a fine tooth comb, literally beating ourselves up over the gloomy outlook that lay before us. Regardless, who could sleep with something like this going on? Sleep would have served no purpose.

The dawn broke early. We had toast. I was ready to throw up if I saw another cup of coffee. Larry wasn't like me. I thought I was being methodical; he defined it as motherly. I thought he was too nonchalant. In truth he had bitten off all his fingernails.

By now there was an all-out search going on. Police were scouring every abandoned building, chasing bums from under local bridges and park benches, making a microscopic search of the city and its suburbs. A kidnapper could move very fast and cover a lot of ground, if there was one.

When the phone rang, I jumped out of my skin. I was at Larry's side instantly straining to hear what was being said on the other end of the wire. I was choking on my heart which felt stuck in my throat.

"Corrinne's dead, isn't she?" I asked but it came out more like a statement of fact.

"They haven't found anything yet," Larry answered, "but they're questioning the janitor. They think he may know something. They'll contact us shortly."

"Shouldn't we go down there?" I queried.

"Not yet. They don't have enough information right now. They're holding him."

"Larry, what about that psychic lady we saw on TV a while back? They say she works with the police all the time in murder cases and stuff like that."

"Honey, please. Don't talk like Corrinne's been murdered. We have to wait and trust the police. We have to be a little patient. I know how you feel. I miss her, too.

But, we can't make ourselves crazy like this. Let's say a prayer together."

I couldn't wait for a prayer to find its way to God's ears. I needed something NOW!

"I want my daughter back, alive. I want to know what's happened." I blurted.

"Things like this happen everyday. We have to give the police whatever it takes."

The day came and went and I wondered if this was going to be over in a little while or was it going to be like one of those Lindbergh cases that took forever to solve? I didn't know if I could live with that kind of suspense. I was too impatient to live through all that.

The next day we were called to the police station. Someone had found a pair of eyeglass frames but they had no lenses. They belonged to Corrinne. We wondered what could possibly have caused the lenses to be missing from their frames. It was too awful to think about what this could mean. I was stunned, stupefied. Depressed was more like it.

The police couldn't give us much information until they had more to go on. They didn't tell us where they found the glass frames but they felt certain they were on the right trail. More waiting. Less coherency when I spoke to Larry. I was starting to sound like some simpering, babbling idiot. If it were he, I don't think I could have put up with that type of behavior. Larry must have been a saint in a three-piece-suit. In truth, he told me he had the same thoughts but he tried to stifle them when I would carry on this way.

The next day the janitor was back on the job, nervous because the police warned him he wasn't to leave town for any reason. If he did, he'd be on a TV alert so fast, he'd live to regret it. He promised to stick around, not talk to anyone. He was warned they were watching him.

He came to work but today he wore a long-sleeved shirt under his denim overalls. Under his sleeve was a large bandage. When they asked him about it, he said he cut himself while fixing some old metal door in the gymnasium.

On the third day police bloodhounds found Corrinne tied up and gagged in a boxcar near the far end of the railroad tracks. She had been there and she wasn't wearing glasses. She identified her abductor as the janitor but she couldn't see him without her glasses. He had put a cloth over her head and chloroformed her so she wouldn't scream.

She said when she came to she couldn't see with the bag over her head and her mouth was taped shut. Her hands were tied behind her and she felt herself being carried somewhere. When they got to the boxcar, she heard a large metal door being pushed aside and the next thing she knew, she was tossed inside and landed on the floor. She didn't have any strength as she was just coming out of the ether so she wasn't able to move very much.

Corrinne laid still for a few minutes to get her bearings. She didn't know where she was or who the man was. When he took off her head covering, it was dark so she couldn't see him. He bent close to her and the glasses fell out of his top pocket. Grabbing for them, she broke the frame and the lenses got crushed underfoot in their struggle.

He loosened one arm, kept the other bent at the elbow and tied up so she wouldn't move it. He told her not to scream if he gave her some water or he might have to kill her.

She drank some of the water from a plastic bottle and then a familiar smell came to her nostrils. It was the smell of the pine cleaner the janitor used to clean the lavatories.

When he was kneeling down beside her, she grabbed the frame with her free hand and managed to gash his arm. He got angry and smacked her and retaped her mouth.

Then he told her he should leave her there to die; that she didn't appreciate that he gave her water. He said he'd come back the next day and that she'd better remain quiet or he might kill her. Then she heard the metal door slide open and shut and he was gone.

She was crying and her mouth hurt from the tape. She felt wet; she had peed her pants.

When the ordeal was over and we had Corrinne back home, we didn't feel safe living in our city. We talked about moving away, another job, a different school. Larry couldn't just up and leave at that time. There were too many obligations to the firm.

Time passed and Corrinne was growing up. She'd been going to a private school and the janitor was sent away to serve a prison term for kidnapping. The publicity didn't help Corrinne's self-esteem. She became withdrawn and she hardly attended any school functions. When Larry's job allowed, we moved to another city and severed all ties to our former life for safety reasons.

Corrinne grew up with her therapist's help and a lot of encouragement from us.

You wouldn't have recognized her when she graduated from high school. She had made the Honor Roll and after several operations to correct her vision, she was wearing the newest discovery in eyewear, prescription contact lenses.

One day she confessed to her Dad and me that the best thing she ever remembered about her "coke bottle glasses" was that they left their indelible mark on her abductor's arm. She said they weren't so bad. They saved her life, after all.

* * * *

Bernice Hamilton has spent her life working with ophthalmologists in the field of retinal diseases and corneal deficiencies. Retirement and her English Sheepdog, Ruggy, keep her busy and content.

GONE IN A MINUTE

HANS HAMMERSCHMIDT III

In Austria Hans' relatives owned a small lodge near the foot of the Alps. In the summer months tourists came to camp, hike, ride horses and swim. Winters were reserved for skiing, ice skating and sleigh rides. This was a very well known resort lodge. Very often the local newspapers would run feature stories and take photos of the lodge and promote the ski area to bring year-round business to the local community. It was a family-owned business that had begun and flourished many years ago. At twenty-four, Hans was already bored with the whole tourist scene.

He wanted to live and work in a big city. He wanted to make and keep friends rather than just see the same occasional faces year after year and make the same small talk day after boring day.

He voiced his feelings several times and almost every time, he wound up in an argument between himself, his father and his grandfather. Traditionally, such businesses were handed down through generations and should have been appreciated for their heritage.

Hans couldn't see it like that and he wanted to be on his own. He promised to finish out the winter season and then he was moving away to work elsewhere. That was final!

The huge lobby held a massive stone fireplace which burned from October until the end of April. Thousands of hot toddies were consumed beside that hearth and many a stolen kiss launched some "fireside fantasies."

Over the huge mantle hung the head of a mountain deer which once weighed in at approximately two-hundred pounds. He was lovingly known as Schnee which means Snow. He was snow white and he had the largest set of antlers this side of the North Pole.

Schnee was a gorgeous specimen and he had beautiful big dark eyes. He also held a secret. The secret was when Schnee was captured, a gunshot wound took out one of his eyes so he was taxidermed with a set of glassies. (No one knew, of course.)

Back-to-back with that monstrous mantle was the wall which separated the lobby from another room, smaller in size, and known by the sign over the door. It read quite simply "Snow View Room." It boasted a glass wall which curved around to offer a breathtaking view of the entire mountain so skiers could be seen from both rooms.

Behind that wall of the lobby and the Snow View Room was a huge bookcase with a storage area over top. It contained an outstanding collection of prized rifles, pistols and swords. It was one of the lodge's most notable treasures because they were valuable remnants of Grandfather's legacy.

During his last winter at the lodge Hans saw there were some new guests to the lodge. Being a charming host, he made certain they were catered to so their vacation would be exemplary.

However, one man seemed noticeably reserved, serious and not very sociable.

He kept to the small group and rarely mingled with other skiers. On party nights he withdrew and stayed on the sidelines as if not to be noticed. He'd usually excuse himself rather early and go to his room taking his drink with him.

It was unreasonable to question the behavior of any guest so Hans ignored it. One night he awakened by the night watchman tapping on his door.

"Sir, I think there's someone prowling around near the lobby. I've looked around and didn't see anyone, yet I heard some little noises so I thought I'd better let you know."

Hans crept downstairs through the service staircase and he saw the remote gentleman sitting in the lobby staring at nothing. Hans waited and watched. Seeing nothing unusual, he returned to his room.

The next day the housekeeper reported one of the locked cases under the desk appeared to be tampered with. That night Hans went down the service stairs to watch.

After nearly an hour, nothing happened. Once again he returned to his room. He was baffled.

Perhaps it was just a coincidence. Still he had an uneasy feeling about the man he'd seen sitting in the lobby the night before.

The next day a considerable sum of the day's Deutsche Marks were missing. The locked case was intact. Hans reported this to his father and they decided not to call in the police yet. After all, who could trace cash even if the police were called in to investigate?

Every night Hans would quietly go downstairs to keep watch. On the night before the new guests were to check out, Hans removed the guns, pistols and swords from their cabinet over the mantle in the Snow View Room. During the night he let himself into the room, climbed the bookcase in his stocking feet and perched himself in the gun cabinet.

Deftly he removed one of Schnee's glass eyes and waited. Around 3 o'clock, just as he suspected, the strange man entered the lobby from the front staircase. Looking around he swiftly made his way to the desk and dropped to his knees out of sight.

Within a short time, Hans heard the lock of the safe being worked. Fearful that the man might have a gun, Hans carefully took a shotgun and made his way toward the desk.

Pointing the gun over the top he yelled for the man to come out or he'd shoot him.

Hans had never been in this type of situation. The thought he might have to kill a man stunned him.

The man jumped up and in a feminine voice shouted, "Don't shoot! Please, don't shoot!"

Hans was so shocked, he almost dropped the rifle. His hands trembled and he cursed himself silently for looking so scared. He was as nervous as a cat in a room full of rockers.

"Who are you? Are you crazy? I'm going to kill you if you don't give up!" Hans shouted.

The figure stood up and as he did so, he took off his hat and a wig. Standing there before Hans was... a woman! A woman dressed as a man and posing as a man, all that time!

Hans was flabbergasted, to say the least. He couldn't comprehend this charade and it made him even more confused. Where were the reporters when you wanted one?

His mind was racing but the words weren't making much sense for either of them. He was as surprised as she at the revelation.

The lady told him her friends knew nothing about her masquerade and they really thought she was a young man. They had become friends recently and they didn't know her very well. She came along with them because she needed money and didn't have a job.

Hans wasn't buying into any of this. When the town's little police force came out, all six of them, there was quite a lot of twittering in the lodge. In town the news traveled fast.

You might think the scandal would have hurt the little lodge's business. But, you know what they say about advertising? Even bad news is still...THE NEWS!

The money was returned, the young lady apprehended and Hans went off in the springtime to live and work in the big city.

As for Schnee, he's keeping an eye out for any future mischief makers.

* * * *

Hans Messerschmidt II left the lodge to his only granddaughter, Elisa, who is Hans III only child. She sold the lodge years ago to live with her husband in the big city where her father lived. She never went back to Snow View in the foothills of Austria.

DUCKS IN A ROW

LAVINIA WEINGARTEN

IN GERMANY THE GIRL who tends the geese is called gansliesel, goose girl. If you're wondering what a goose girl does to keep busy, it means taking a herd of geese out to pasture for fresh grass. It also means getting them home safely, making certain they don't get chased by a lurking wolf for his dinner.

Lavinia had a way of singing and whistling at the geese. Since they were raised with her from babies, they responded to her voice. It was quite a sight to see her with a tall staff leading eighty or a hundred geese as they followed her around.

Some were very affectionate and would fly into her lap when she was seated on the ground. The littler ones would stay very close to her so she could feed them grain by hand. The older, more aggressive males automatically grew into herders and would help protect the females and their babies.

When Lavinia would whistle that it was time to return home, she'd call out to the ducks, "Gans, gans, gans" (Geese, geese, geese) and they'd all begin marching with her in a row as she took up the lead. The bigger, taller males, distinguishable by their greyish color, would help her round up the others. Together they made their way back down the low mountain path toward the farmyard and into the barn where they slept. The barn door had an opening through which the ducks went in and out on their own.

Ducks have a strange language of their own and various "quacks" to communicate.

Lavinia imitated them and they seemed to have a clear rapport. For example, if two males began fighting over a female, Lavinia scolded them and they'd crouch down until she allowed them to get up by talking sweetly to them.

If a mother duck was pecking at her baby and making the baby "peep," Lavinia would take the baby in her arms and walk with it and the mother was made to walk on the edge of the herd. Truly, here was a little schoolhouse group of ducks and their teacher and most of the time, they minded her.

Lavinia lived with her parents and a much older sister who was already married. Her sister's job was tending the henhouse and helping birth the new calves. Her mother managed the household and her father and brother-in-law raised a few small crops. The work was shared by all and, even in the worst winters, the family always had enough food.

There was never a need to be fearful of intruders as their land was a long way from the town. The only people who came passing through were neighboring farmers and the families they knew. It was a wholesome life and somewhat calm.

They attended church and some social events in summer and fall which carried them over the winter months. If a girl was to meet a fella, summer was most probable.

In the fall the grain was piled high in the barn and loft to keep for the entire winter's rations of bread, grain cereal and animal feed. It was not to be wasted.

Lavinia's bedroom looked out toward the barn. One night she awoke and she sat straight up in her bed. Beyond the whistling wind, she thought she was awakened by some strange muffled sounds outside her side of the house. At first, it didn't seem like much so she went back to sleep. Shortly after, she heard the sounds again so she got out of bed and went to the window. There was a shuffling sound coming from the barn but she thought perhaps it was the cow who was heavy with calf. It wasn't her time to deliver but Lavinia thought the cow may have been somewhat restless. She'd look into that in the morning.

The next day Lavinia's father came in from the barn looking perturbed. He'd been out to harness up the mules and he said he saw several small trails of grain on the barn floor. He told Lavinia to clean it up and check to see if any bags had been broken. Then he went out to the fields with his son-in-law.

Lavinia thought it was strange that the ducks would tear into the grain sacks. They were not usually destructive so she gently scolded them for trashing the grain and went about her business. That morning the ducks seemed agitated when she took them out to pasture. Lavinia took a head count and they were all there so what was the problem, she wondered.

Lavinia went into the storage cellar to get some dried meat for her lunch and she noticed that the sausage strings were not all the same length. Funny, she didn't recall Mutter cooking sausages lately. I can't keep track of every little thing, she thought. Looking further, she caught a glimpse of the cheese bin – something was missing.

It can't be a wolf taking down the sausages and getting into the cheese bin. She hurried toward the house to tell her Mutter that sausages, cheese and even some apples were misplaced. Muttie denied using sausages or cheese for cooking lately and she said she'd tell Papa when he came in from the field.

For the next few nights Lavinia didn't hear any sounds or see any loose grain on the barn floor the mornings after. Thinking all was back to normal, she dismissed the worry. The ducks, however, still didn't seem very settled and Lavinia wondered about that.

The following week Lavinia's father and brother-in-law returned from town and said they had heard there was a thief in the local area. Some farmers complained of losing things in their larders. Lavinia's father decided to lock the barn and cellar doors at night just to be on the safe side. Lavinia was restless that entire first night. She looked out at the barn but seeing nothing unusual, she finally went to sleep just before dawn.

The next day Lavinia gathered her ducks for the pasture. Today was going to be a long day so she went to the cellar to pick out some dried sausage and cheese for her lunch. She was shocked to see that once again, it appeared some sausage links were missing and the cheese bin was short another cheese ball.

Returning from the field, Lavinia decided to do a little investigating on her own. That night she stayed up and she stayed dressed. She put on a coat and snug hat and went out on the porch and waited. There it was again, those muffled sounds coming from the barn. Quickly, quietly she went back inside and woke up her brother-in-law, Friedrich. After she told him what she'd heard, he grabbed a horse whip and he and Lavinia tiptoed out to the barn.

They moved quietly toward the small side door and crept inside. Just at the middle of the loft ladder was the intruder with arms full of sausages and cheese from the cellar.

Lavinia whistled and yelled to her ducks, "GANS, GANS, GANS!" and at once, nearly the entire flock of ducks went flying around the room.

Friedrich snapped the whip at the man's feet and Lavinia began to whistle to the ducks who were flying all around the ladder and leaping up toward the bandit. He was as surprised as they and unable to keep his balance, he tumbled off the ladder to the floor.

At once the huge grey ducks were all around him pecking at him with a vengeance. Lavinia continued to whistle and yell to the ducks, "GANS, GANS, GANS!" Now they were in a frenzy jumping on top of the man and pecking at his head and pulling his hair as if they understood what was happening. They nipped at his arms, legs and belly as the man yelled out, grimacing in pain. The ducks were having a field day showing off how masterful they could be at the command of their ganseliesel. Friedrich tied up the man with his horse whip and Lavinia ran to fetch her Papa.

The next day the thief was taken into town and handed over to the police. The news spread quickly. Lavinia was so proud that her ducks did such a splendid job apprehending a thief.

For an entire week Lavinia praised her ducks and she promised never to scold them again. What a surprise it was when a story appeared in the local paper that a posted reward would be granted to Freulein Lavinia Weingarten now known as the Diva and her Duck Detectives.

* * * *

The **Weingarten's** have lived in America for many years. Over their mantle is a huge picture of Lavinia walking through the barnyard with all her ducks in a row.

WHERE THERE'S SMOKE

TERRELL URBANIK

MRS. URBANIK could never figure out why her twins chose such dangerous careers: policeman and fireman. Why couldn't they just be regular people with regular jobs? she often asked herself. What's wrong with being an insurance salesman or realtor?

They made a good, predictable paycheck every week and they didn't leave their mothers and wives at home turning gray wondering if this day would be their last on earth.

From the time the twins were small, Rita Urbanik spent a good portion of everyday worrying about their futures. Terrell and Dana were a handful to raise. Bursting with energy and appetites to match, those boys ran her ragged while they were growing up. Rita should have been pencil-thin but such was not the case.

Rita was a short, fleshy gal with a happy heart, soul and personality. It didn't take much to make her smile or make her cry; she was that tender-hearted. She doted on her family as her mother had done while Rita was growing up.

Rita cooked up the best pot of kielbasa in the neighborhood and she wondered if the praise she received wasn't just a patronizing excuse for her to invite someone to sit at her abundant table. Whatever it was, it made her heart feel good when she was feeding someone. The Bible said it's the best display of absolute love.

The twins were used to hearty meals and Rita always believed that a happy kitchen is the heart of the family unit. Terrell and Dana took up Mom's good natured ways and they were a blessing to the neighborhood.

Dana was the robust twin and all he ever talked about was becoming a fireman. One day his Dad brought home an old beat-up fireman's hat and gave it to Dana. From that day, Dana wanted to put out every single fire, including the one on Mom's little gas range.

One day Rita was heating up a small pot of water for coffee and Dana decided to put out the fire so he poured the pot of water onto the range putting out the gas flame. Rita smelled the gas fumes and came running into the kitchen. She scolded Dana and he cried. All he wanted to do was put out the flames. Score another gray hair.

Terrell's dream was to be a policeman and catch every criminal this side of Alcatraz. From the time he saw his first Elliot Ness TV series of "The Untouchables," Terrell wanted to be a crimestopper with a .38 revolver in a shoulder holster. Terrell was tall and slim like Robert Stack's Elliott Ness. He'd imitate Ness' swaggering, confident walk, look you square in the eyes and say, " 'Take 'em downtown, boys and book 'em.' " Then he'd crack up laughing. Realizing the twins were not heading into desk job careers, Rita went to church every Sunday and prayed for their safety.

By the time Dana and Terrell were into their respective careers, Rita got used to their hair-raising stories about the fires they fought and the lives they saved. It was always nerve-wracking for her to think her sons were in such life-and-death situations. She knew this was their calling and Rita had a tremendous faith in the Almighty. She was convinced that if God wanted her boys to live a long life, they would have His blessings.

One day Terrell was working on the far side of the city when he got a call on his two-way radio. There was a fire in Dana's district so Terrell and his partner went flying across town to see if they could help. On the two-way Terrell was getting an account of the fire which had broken out in a rundown neighborhood, probably from a space heater that had been defective or overheated. It wasn't unusual this time of year.

Some of the lower-income tenement houses didn't have air-conditioning or adequate heat so the occupants often used floor model space heaters during the winter months.

Many lives were threatened or lost unnecessarily in fires but there wasn't much anyone could do to improve those conditions. City politicians were busy doing things that dug into the city's budgets for what they felt were more worthy causes such as replacing old trash barrels with newer ones and other unimportant projects.

Once in the neighborhood, Terrell and his partner could hear the screaming sirens of several fire trucks and ambulances coming from all directions. Their eerie music always made his stomach churn and his palms began to sweat in spite of the cold temperature.

Swerving around the corner, Terrell saw the foreboding scene. Smoke billowed out of an upper floor window. Screams were filling the cold, night air and a furnace-like wall of flames came belching from the building. Hoses sprayed the facade as firemen were already lowering bodies out of windows and other people were attempting to jump into the safety nets below. It was a living nightmare in third dimension.

The Red Cross was handing out blankets and hot coffee. Ambulances were poised at both ends of the burning building as paramedics lined up gurneys and stretchers to remove victims to a local hospital. A Salvation Army bus was standing nearby as a refuge from the cold. Volunteers were comforting the survivors.

Looking up Terrell saw people standing in window frames, frantically waving for help, a few already in flames jumping out with little or nothing on their backs. One baby, dropped by its mother into the arms of a policeman, had already perished from the smoke.

Terrell recalled how often he'd heard Dana say he never knew which was worse: being the victims or the survivors.

By now ambulances were racing in and out of the street transporting as many people as possible in the shortest time. Behind him Terrell saw two TV station trucks recording the incident for the late night news. Newspaper reporters were making cell phone reports to the City Desk as the morning presses were already rolling.

The street had a little bit of slush by the curbs and Terrell cursed the wintry wind that kept fanning the flames in all directions. Overhead the sky was filled with thick, black smoke that kept curling upwards from the flames that kissed the night sky.

"Yeah, Kiss of Death," thought Terrell sarcastically.

Just then he caught sight of Dana who was coming toward him. Dana looked like a moving statue in his high boots, fire coat and hat. Terrell's heart filled with pride for his brother who was highly respected in his station for meritorious service. He thought firefighting was such an imperiled occupation, he queried as to whether or not there was a bizarre kind of satisfaction those daredevils got from endangering themselves so often. Perhaps it was a hand-to-hand battle with the Devil himself to prove who could win.

At his side now, Dana shouted above the noise, "It's hell in there but I gotta go back in. Looks like we're gonna be here all night. Can't tell how many are left inside."

"Terrell, check the house when you get in and let Eileen know I'm okay. She'll be worried when she hears how bad this one is."

Terrell nodded his assent. Dana left to go into the inferno.

In the dark Terrell's watch read 1:17 a.m. The fire had been going strong for quite a while and it might be several hours before they got it under control. No telling how many lives would be lost in that much time. Terrell's partner, Marvin, was working with other policemen and Terrell wished he had six hands to help at times like this.

In the face of utter chaos, it's an amazing thing to see how so many people work with such swiftness and coordination. Every man and woman was an integral part of this unrehearsed performance pulling their weight with no intention other than to save lives.

Here was a place where prejudice, money or status had no meaning. People from all walks of life were selflessly working their hearts out to bring solace and calm to bedlam.

On the ground adults were clinging to each other, crying, screaming and praying aloud. There were hundreds of people on a set which would have stood the test of time if someone were to use this for a major motion picture. The only difference was this was gruesomely real and the lives of the so-called actors were truly in jeopardy.

Between praying and cursing under his breath, Terrell felt the intense heat as the wind blew the smoke and flames in his direction. The stream of bodies being taken out of the building seemed perpetual; no one knew exactly how many more were still inside.

There wouldn't be an exact number until the fire was out and an account was taken.

Several victims were already being removed to a local shelter and more buses were being filled. Neighbors came out to help and took several victims into their homes. Two local priests stood by the ambulances giving last rites and blessings to the dead or injured.

From inside the building could be heard the sound of collapsing walls and more screaming as people were being thrown into the burning rubble or trapped under it. Suddenly an ear-splitting explosion burst upon the calamitous scene. In all probability one or more oil burners had exploded and one huge portion of the facade fell into itself.

It was impossible to distinguish one fireman from another at a distance. Terrell grabbed a firecoat from the shoulders of a fireman seated near the Red Cross station which was treating his arm. Pulling the hat onto his own head, he yanked up the collar and ran. He darted toward the building against the orders of the Fire Chief who was barking directions left and right.

"You can't go in there! You'll only get caught! Stay here, stay here!" he yelled.

A strong arm tried to hold him back but Terrell broke free and ran for the building.

If God wants me to live....if God wants Dana to live, I'll know soon enough, he prayed. Either Terrell was about to meet the Devil or meet his Maker, he didn't know which, but he did know that God was watching this whole scenario. Why then wouldn't He stop it?

Terrell knew only that Dana was in there and he wasn't going to let his other half die without making an attempt to reach him. He knew Dana was doing all he could to help so many people. This time it was Dana who needed help. Terrell was never so scared as he was right now. He'd faced murderers with guns and took his chances, but this... This was another ball game. For the first time Terrell realized that firefighters had nerves of steel or no nerves at all to feel anything but a drive to conquer these fires.

Once inside, Terrell was astounded when confronted by the awesome danger he faced. He didn't have boots, gloves, mask or training for this. He felt stupid and remorseful that maybe now he'd put someone's else life in danger to save his. He hated his impulsive choice but here he was and he couldn't go back.

"DANA! DANA! DAAAAANAAAA!" Terrell knew his voice couldn't be heard over the din. He also remembered that many people die from super-heated air which lurks about two feet above the floor surface. He knew if he crouched down, it would slow down his attempt to find Dana. What the hell was he thinking when he did such a dumb thing?

Turning around only once or twice could make one lose their direction as nothing was distinguishable now. Walls were crumbled, flames and smoked blocked out the view of passageways and exits. Terrell cursed himself over and over and knew the only thing left was for him to get out NOW!

His nostrils filled with the smell of gassy fumes. His eyes and face burned fiercely from the intense heat and he felt himself choking. He gasped and instead of feeling some relief, he realized he'd sucked in more smoke. He was retching and his lungs were closing in. He couldn't touch anything as he'd already burned his hands more than once.

Somehow he made his way toward a window but before he could get there, the entire room caved in around him. Instinctively he threw his hands over his head in a protective manner but he felt something strike his back and he was thrown to the floor.

Flames were all around him. He felt weak and overcome with a burning sensation as he realized his shoes were on fire. He couldn't figure whether he should try to crawl or stand up. He tried to yell but his throat was so parched, nothing came out. He'd been hit by a falling timber and he thought it may have broken a back rib. A sharp, needle-like pain shot through his spine and he gripped his rib cage and hollered in agony.

He thought he yelled for God to help him but he didn't hear himself saying a word. Painfully, Terrell crawled over the rough floor which had an enormous gaping hole in the middle where everything had fallen through to the ground below.

There is was, a window. He prayed it was an escape so he tried to get around the circumference of the flooring which was hanging suspended, its rafters reaching downward like long, slender helpless arms. The timbers had been deteriorating with age. They looked so eerie as if trying to reach out for help while they were slowly being consumed by the flames. Before he could reach the window, he felt something strike his shoulder. It was at that moment Terrell passed out.

Someone's moaning. Omigod! Where am I? Terrell opened his eyes to a very dark room. At first he couldn't remember anything and then...

"Hello, Terrell. I'm Helen, your night nurse."

A soft voice in the darkened room told him he was still alive. He tried to move and pain went coursing through his spine. His leg felt completely numb. He let out a long moan.

He heard some ticking noises but he could barely make out the apparatus by his bed that was checking his vital signs. The nurse standing beside him was hooking up a bottle to his existing IV line. She methodically stuck a thermometer in his mouth, checked his blood pressure reading, made notes, checked bandages, uncovered him and looked at the body wrappings on his rib cage, checked the bandaged feet, the legs, rolled him gently on his side, stuck a needle in his buttock, rolled him back and tucked him in. She never blinked an eye.

"You've been here since yesterday morning and you've had a long sleep. You're in the ICU/Trauma Center. You've been in surgery for a broken rib and some pretty nasty burns. Your doctor will see you in the morning. I'll be here all night checking in on you regularly, now that you're conscious."

She spoke softly, compassionately, like she was reading off a set of rules, yet her voice was gentle and caring and her touch was like a feather.

It wasn't until then Terrell realized his leg was bound up. He looked down there.

"Oh, my! You also got a broken leg when you were hit by some falling debris. It'll be a while before you start feeling better but you're doing okay for now."

She went on. "Terrell, your hair was burned off and you have some head burns and abrasions. Please don't try to scratch anywhere. You're medicated and we don't want any infections, ok? Luckily your brother pulled you out just in time."

Nurse Helen came close to Terrell's side. She looked like an angel all in white.

"Suck on this little bit of ice; it'll keep your mouth from feeling so dry. You were very dehydrated when you came in but you're better as of this minute. Your Mother and brother were here to see you yesterday but..."

Her voice trailed off. Terrell's mind began to recall what had happened yesterday.

Terrell didn't need to hear anymore. He was safe. Dana was safe. That's all that mattered. Huge tears rolled down his cheeks.

He closed his eyes and said silently, "Thank you, God."

"Is there anything I can do for you before I leave?" Helen asked.

Terrell motioned slightly for Helen to come near. At his side, he whispered hoarsely to her.

"Please tell Dana I never meant for this to happen. I didn't realize until I was trapped how bad it was in there. If I don't talk to someone, I'll never forgive myself."

Helen drew up a chair so Terrell could relate his story of the fire. Tears rolled down his bandages and Helen dabbed at her eyes as he detailed the gory event. Now and again Terrell broke into wrenching sobs as remorse tore at his soul. Helen gently wiped away his tears but she let him go on for she knew this catharsis was lifting a burden from him.

Early the next morning, Rita and Dana were in Terrell's room when he awoke. They stopped in early to say 'hello' and that they'd be returning later that evening when he might be feeling up to seeing them for a few minutes. Rita kissed her son and left the room. Dana took Terrell's hand. Terrell looked up and saw Dana's eyes were misty. Dana tried to smile but he looked extremely tired and worn out. He whispered lovingly,

"Terrell, you dumb sucker, if you weren't my brother, I'd knock you out!"

Terrell promised himself he'd tell Dana the whole story when he was well enough and able to forgive himself for the dangers he created for the others. Dana told Terrell that the thump he felt on his shoulder was when he dropped a hand on him to pull his from the burning wreckage. He was already unconscious then. Dana knew this was not the time to scold. Instead he bent down and kissed his brother on the forehead and looked long into his tearful eyes.

He chided, "All I wanted you to do was call Eileen and you forgot to do THAT!"

Just like Dana, Terrell thought. It's no wonder everyone loves this guy.

Dana smiled, "You just be a good boy now, and mind what the folks here tell you. You're gonna be one sick pup for a while but we'll get you back on your feet so the guys down at the precinct can beat you up later. See ya tomorrow."

Dana left the room and Terrell let himself drift into a long and peaceful sleep.

That same night Terrell went into cardiac arrest from trauma aftershock. (Nurse Helen related Terrell's story to Dana after Terrell slept away.)

* * * *

Rita Urbanik was so happy to learn about Angel Parent Memories. She said this has brought her newfound peace and harmony with the universe. Soon she will begin working to promote its mission to help other Angel Parents.

BEACH BOYS

JOEL PERCY

LIVING IN THE Pacific Northwest we had to take advantage of every sunny day. If I only whispered the word "beach" the boys would begin jumping around like grasshoppers. Show me a kid who didn't love the beach...

We were at Salt Creek, about fifteen miles from our home in Port Angeles. The beaches were seldom crowded because the water was hardly ever warm. May be a dozen people had the nerve to show up. I recall going to the beach and roasting our hot dogs and beans in a downpour. From there we went to the Elwah river and fished. Afterwards we headed to the Hurricane Ridge in the Olympic Mountains (above Pt. Angeles) to play in the snow. We did that all on the same day.

One day in mid-summer I packed a hamper with some sandwiches, potato salad, juice and cookies. Joel had his friends, Don and Tim Larson, with him. Joel and Don were best buddies.

At fourteen years of age, Joel didn't care much for dragging little Todd around and his friends always told Todd to get lost. Todd's eight-year-old hero-worship for his big brother Joel, was paramount. He wanted to do everything Joel could in spite of his age.

It was a perfect beach day. Lots of driftwood, fancy shells and other things made it fun for the little ones to build fancy sand castles. The outgoing tide left an excellent tide pool for the younger children to play in and today the pickin's were even better. This day the tide pool was about five feet deep, just right for a raft, a dive and a swim.

The bigger boys had put together a raft from found items on the sand and they held it together with seaweed and kelp. It was like having their personal pirate ship.

Todd began doggie-paddling in the tide pool to reach the raft as I looked on from the distance. Duane, my little son, and I were building a castle and decorating it with fancy shells. Oddly enough I'd never learned to swim though I lived most of my life near the water. I made certain the boys would have that pleasure and could swim like little fish.

Everyone seemed to be having a lot of fun laughing and splashing in the pool. What I never heard was Todd pleading with Joel's friends to not throw him into the water.

Suddenly someone shouted out Todd's name. Looking up, all I could see were Todd's hands flapping at the water but his body was not in view. Grabbing Duane I ran toward the pool and just then I saw Joel dive in and bring little Todd to the surface. He was coughing and spitting but safe. Joel had saved Todd's life.

Today Todd remembers and says, "If it weren't for Joel." Then he says quietly,

"Thanks, bro."

* * * *

Sandra Ruzicka has championed her life as a single parent raising three sons. She cast several bottles with poems inside into the Pacific Ocean on May 31, 2003. Another bottle dropped by a friend into the Gulf of Mexico reached Ft. Lauderdale seven months later.

With a poem she added this note:

> *"This bottle has been put adrift in memory of a loved one, Joel Percy, in honor of his birth date. We hope this bottle will make it to the far reaches of the earth for his memory is in here."*

This has been Joel's story.

Author's note: *This story was so unusual and newsworthy. It was written by Rafael A. Olmeda of the South Florida Sun Sentinel and appeared on the Associated Press wire.*

SECTION TWO

* * * *

Love

A KISS TO LAST FOREVER

PAUL D'AMICO

THE ARMY WAS PREPARING to ship thousands of troops to Beirut that year. Like all mothers, I was worried about my young son, Paul, who had enlisted the year before. I knew there was a strong possibility he'd be going and there was the chance I would not see him before he left. Worse was the thought I might never see him again. I tried not to talk about it because whenever someone asked me about him, I'd begin to cry.

Paul was a great kid, barely nineteen and full of life. The youngest of three boys, Paul was a little quiet but he'd often say, "Don't take my niceness for weakness." He wasn't one to let people push him around simply because he had a big heart. He was a soft touch for a hard luck story and he would help anyone he could.

Paul had already gone to Fork Union Military Academy in Virginia, one of the nation's highest academies and I was extremely proud of him. He was involved in many things while he was there, including Golden Gloves boxing and soccer. He even learned to speak French. Foreign languages came easily to him. He had picked up Italian when, as a young teenager, he spent a summer in Italy.

Paul called me one day to tell me the enlisted men were going elsewhere, not everyone was going to Beirut. I breathed a sigh of relief. Maybe he didn't have to go to Beirut after all, I hoped. The news reports were full of stories about the nuclear reactor plant that was destroyed and some of our Marines who were killed. My heart bled for the mothers of those young men, boys as they were.

Several days passed and no word from Paul. I wondered if some troops were being shipped out sooner. Maybe Paul didn't have a chance to call to say 'good-bye'. There was nothing I could do but pray, wait and pray some more.

Mother's Day was approaching and, in an effort to lift my spirits, my children insisted I go out to dinner with them for the occasion. I didn't have much enthusiasm. I always wanted to stay close to the phone in the event Paul might call me.

Glancing at the calendar I saw many days I'd checked off. I realized I was feeling tired all the time because I had so many sleepless nights. Sleeping with one eye open, as my mother used to say. If the phone rang and it turned out to be a wrong number, I'd just fall apart because it wasn't Paul calling. Then I'd feel angry.

With a certain amount of trepidation I went through the motions and dressed to go out for dinner, all the while double-guessing myself as to whether or not I should.

I supposed everyone was weary of hearing my complaints and what good would it do?

I took one last quick look in the mirror, turning my head this way and that. What was I looking for? Oh, yes, another wrinkle on my brow. Another little bag under the eyes.

"I'm going to grow old before my time if I don't stop frowning," I said aloud.

Besides, Paul wouldn't think very much of me if I kept on like this. After all, he was alive and well. That threw a little guilt trip on me.

I decided to wear something more glamorous. I pulled out my grape Versace jumpsuit. It was one of Paul's favorite outfits on me. Whenever I wore it, he'd say I looked so good, he'd take me out on a date, but he was too old for me and we'd laugh about that.

I touched up my eyes with concealer, stroked on a brighter lipstick and lavished on some Dolce and Gabanna perfume. There, that was better. I was starting to look like me again.

I grabbed the camera at the last minute. Paul would want to see photos of everyone.

In the restaurant I tried to appear calm and happy because my children were all around me and for that I was thankful. Yet when my heart gave a sigh, it came out of my lips. We made small talk carefully tip-toeing around Paul's obvious absence.

My daughter, Cindy, tried to lift my spirits and asked, "Mother, if you could have just one wish for Mother's Day, what would it be?" (Need she ask?)

There was just one answer: "I wish Paul were here to celebrate this day with me."

Cindy made a broad gesture like a magician and said, "POOF!" Out of nowhere, my handsome son, Paul, was standing beside me with a dozen pink roses in his hands. I looked up and he bent down and placed a tender, loving kiss on my lips which I shall never, ever forget. It was truly a kiss to last forever.

—Carmen D'Amico

* * * *

Carmen D'Amico has been a professional speaker most of her life when she wasn't involved in other entrepreneurial pursuits. She has contributed writings in several books. Carmen is the designer of the Angel Parent pin which was the dream for this book. Her audio books bring these stories to life with tenderness and spirituality. Formerly a look-alike for Elizabeth Taylor, Carmen helped benefits raise a million dollars for AIDS research. Carmen loves to travel on cruise ships where she has lectured for several years. She has called Ft. Lauderdale, Florida her home for the last 35 years.

THE WEDDING

KATIA LAPINSKI

"OH, SVEN, I love you so much. When I grow up, I'm going to marry you."

"Then let's make a promise that no matter what happens, we won't marry anyone else."

That was the vow taken by Miss Katia Lapinski, age six, and Mr. Sven Anton, age seven.

Sven gave Katia a sweet little kiss on her pouty cherubic lips and the promise was sealed. They said they would never tell anyone but that they would let nothing or no one come between them.

All through school, whenever you saw Katia, you saw Sven. They walked home together, played together and shared dreams of their future careers together.

Sven's father was an excellent carpenter and he wanted his son to have a military career. Katia's father was a violinist and he wanted Katia to become a concert pianist. Their destinies would take them worlds apart; however, at six and seven, who thinks of things like that?

Katia spent day after day practicing the piano. Her parents couldn't afford a piano of their own so they rented an old piano from an elderly spinster who lived a few miles away. Katia's father, Horst, never made much money. He didn't come to the United States until he was a grown man so he had gotten a rather late start in life. Katia's mother was a passive woman who was content to remain in the background giving to Katia what little encouragement she could.

Katia's older brother, Johann, left home right after high school and went to work in another city. He never cared much for rural communities; he was cosmopolitan by nature.

Horst liked Sven as a person but he felt Sven hadn't the sterling qualities for a girl like Katia. Her father wanted Katia to marry a musician and carry on the old world tradition of a musical family.

Their growing up was like most young people but, for Katia and Sven, the reputation they had as a steady couple did not win favor with Horst as his young daughter blossomed and prepared for her social life to include dating and school trips.

Horst began to see Sven as a threat to his daughter's future career and the thought unnerved him. He subtlely arranged for Katia to be booked for recitals and concerts as much as time would permit so that she would find little time for Sven. With luck Katia might even meet another man who would capture her fancy and whisk her away to a better lifestyle than Sven could offer. Marriage to a man with a military career might take her around the world, but it would injure her career in the long run.

Sven's father's influence was unyielding and the pressure for Sven to have a military career was paramount in his father's mind. Driven by the thought that the military would provide his son with every possible opportunity for a career with a guaranteed life income, he prepped his son by sending him to military academies, summer camps and a stint in the Army Reserves.

Katia and Sven renewed their childhood vows and wrote to each other faithfully, detailing every minute of their lives to keep the other stocked with up-to-date news.

Sven had a weekend pass with several of his buddies who took him out to celebrate his birthday. Being one of the guys meant not holding back for the sake of good manners. Sven did not want to seem unappreciative when the guys plowed him with drinks to celebrate his birthday, his love for Katia, his progress in the Reserves and every other reason to have Sven inhale one scotch after another. He was feeling no pain and they were all having a plastering jolly time.

Sauntering up to Sven in a skin-tight red dress with the most outrageous stiletto heels a pair of legs could kick the tail off a brass monkey, a young woman named Maxie was the icing on Sven's birthday cake. Paid for by his buddies, Maxie's job was to unfurl Sven's potency and show him the secrets of the wildest sex he would ever experience in his bachelor boyhood soon lost.

Sven was too drunk to care and the thought of a nice soft bed right now sounded very appealing to him. From where he stood staring at a luscious pair of boobs that looked like the biggest serving of French vanilla ice cream he had ever seen, all he could wonder was how they would taste if in fact they were ice cream.

He didn't remember much after that except that once in a while he saw those boobs in the shadows of a soft lamplight hovering over him as the bed beneath him rocked to and fro.

His head was about to split. He felt sweaty and vulnerable. Everything seemed hazy.

One minute those boobs were above him and next thing he knew they were under him and that's when he finally passed out.

He woke up on his Army bed still not knowing how he got there or what happened the night before. His head was the size of a watermelon and just as heavy and his stomach....

Let's not talk about how his stomach felt. He smelled of scotch and cigarette smoke and with that, he fell back to sleep and didn't come to until late that afternoon.

Katia's letters became less frequent as her busy schedule allowed little time for writing. By the same token, Sven's responses were less and less interesting as he was spending more time with the guys on weekends and there wasn't anything to write home about anyhow.

Katia began touring and, when her father landed her a contract for a series of concerts, Katia couldn't refuse. It was her first great opportunity to begin the concert circuit and launch her musical career at the Philharmonic. Whether or not they suspected, it was the beginning of an end for Katia and Sven.

Sometimes several weeks would pass before Katia would receive mail because Sven was stationed in Europe or somewhere else and she was not able to get her mail while on the road tour. It was probably not so surprising when Katia got news from a friend back home that Sven had married a girl he met in Europe and they moved to another city while he was still in the service.

Katia was busy so she permitted her father to chart the course of her dating career. When he introduced her with great accolades to a concert violinist, it seemed only natural that the two of them should date.

An uninspired match was made and within less than two years, Katia married Sam and they played in the same orchestra and traveled together. Life held very few surprises for them.

Over the years, Sven and Katia had often thought of each other but circumstances never designed their astral charts to intercept one another. Life went on with little excitement and few fireworks. There wasn't time for a family at first; but, several years later when Katia was thirty-seven, she found out she was pregnant so she decided it was time for a sabbatical. She took time off to have her little daughter and Sam traveled without her from then on.

Katia's child was not a healthy baby and she required constant care due to a damaged liver. During one episode, Katia's baby was in trouble. While she sat waiting in the hospital emergency room, Katia's father came to tell her that Sam's tour bus had been in a crash during a severe rainstorm and some of the passengers were killed. Katia didn't need a list of names to tell her she had just become a widow. She was so drained over the baby's illness, Katia couldn't even shed a tear. All she could feel was a dry lump in her chest that wouldn't find its release in a torrent of tears. Katia let her father drive her home and she fell into a sleep state of exhaustion.

In the months that followed, Katie walked around in a hollow-eyed trance. There was little hope for the baby's survival so she closed her reality stratum, sealed off her emotions and moved about like a mummy to insulate herself from the impending event of her baby's death.

During the years that followed, Katia immersed herself in an indigo fog of convenient forgetfulness, picking up her concert tours with the mechanics of an automaton.

One opening night in Denmark, Katia returned to her dressing-room to be greeted by an enormous bouquet of flowers with an inscription that read: "I am twenty years late but someone taught me it is never too late to start over."

Looking up at the mirror she saw a familiar face behind her. Sven stood with a half smile on his face, hoping she would respond favorably. For the first time in years, Katia's heart opened its eyes to see the color of joy once again.

In was near midnight when they left the little apres-theater café and by then, many plans for their future were already put into place. Sven had been divorced and he heard that Katia was living alone once again. Destiny was playing her hand to favor their future together. At last Katia would have the beautiful wedding she had always dreamed of and Sven would be there at her side. It was never too late for new beginnings.

Back in the states they spent every waking hour rejuvenating their hearts in a loving symphony set to the music of their love. It was as if twenty years had vanished.

They chose a little country church with just a handful of close friends around them. In Katia's eyes she felt the entire universe was testament to their long-awaited fulfillment of marriage. The ceremony was simple, the vows profound. They could not wait to begin their new life together. Now there was nothing or noone to stop them and they would be united in their hearts and minds 'til the end of time.

They sped off toward the mountains where they would begin their heart's dream. Up and up the winding road they drove as if reaching for the heavens above that blessed their union. Katia was never happier to be alive than she was at this very moment.

The little gold band on her left finger was her most cherished possession right now. How she wanted to shout it from the mountaintop. She looked down at the little innocent flowers she held in her hands. She would press them in book for time immemorial, she thought. How she loved this man. She promised herself she would do everything to make this marriage one of adventure and joy.

Perhaps it wasn't too late to have another child, hers and Sven's. They might even buy a little bed-and-breakfast where they could work together and pretend they were guests on their own premises. Oh, what a fabulous life it will be! She let her mind run wild with anticipation. Nothing could ever, ever come between them. Nothing could ever mar her joy.

Katia talked and laughed with great affection about their sweet little wedding ceremony. The day was so perfect and with the top down, she could see the tall trees that were growing out of the mountainside. The air was crisp and sweet with the smell of nature itself. Far below the world was a wonderland of farms and orchards and streams. Now and then a bird called out to them. Sven stopped the car and got out to pick some flowers for Katia along the side of the road. She got out and watched from above as Sven picked wildflowers from a parapet eight feet from the ledge where she stood.

Without warning the little convertible began rolling backward quietly. Katia was so busy taking pictures of Sven, she never noticed the Volkswagen as it gained momentum. By the time she wanted to step out of its path, the car was blocking her way to safety, pushing her over the edge without a prayer. When the little car rolled over the mountainside, there wasn't a sound to be heard.

Horrified Sven watched as he stood helpless on the ledge below. For several seconds there was nothing to be heard until the car demolished itself in a heap and turned over before coming to a stop...a dead stop.

Echoing from the valley below, Sven could hear the tolling of the bells from the little wedding chapel in the valley.

* * * *

Today Katia's mother, **Ana**, wears Katia's wedding ring on the third finger of her right hand. Beside her are the flowers that she pressed in a book which once belonged to Katia.

GYPSY TAMBOURINE

MEDINA BOROSHENKO WILLIAMS

"Love is the closest a human can get to knowing how an angel feels inside."
—Barb Mark & Trudy Griswold
The Angelspeake Storybook

HER MOTHER AND FATHER were from Romania, gypsies as they were known to be. Her father played an accordion, her mother was a belly dancer. Medina just sat on the sidelines and clapped her hands to the music and the frenzy of the dance.

At times her mother would dance with a huge snake draped around her body and the audience was totally entranced. Other times she danced with tambourines, their tiny cymbals chinking with the slap of her hand as the tempo accelerated. She danced wildly and her skirts would shiver as the fringe and tassels whirled in the wake of her exotic gyrations. Her silky black hair hung to her waist and it flowed with her body and the music. She was a vision of grace and erotica all in one.

Medina loved the way her mother's costumes sparkled under the colored lights making her look like a rainbow flashing before everyone's eyes. Oh, she was so beautiful. She watched as her mother floated around with her gossamer veils surrounding her like they were spun from the ocean's foam. They sparkled and twinkled like millions of stars.

Medina loved her mother with all her heart. She dreamed of growing up to be just like her. Medina saw the same shows a thousand times and each time was always like a new experience to her. From the earliest days of memory, Medina recalled holding a little tambourine and dancing like her mother.

But Medina's mother had other plans for her pretty little daughter. She wanted Medina to become educated and get far away from show business. Living on the road was often a difficult life and she felt Medina had chances for a much greater future.

Medina's father would repair the tambourine with little pieces of tin when they began to fall apart. It never sounded quite the same but noone noticed the difference.

One year the family was in California on a road show and they were appearing in a circus tent at a summertime fair. They had been doing the show for a few nights but this night was different. It had been raining very hard and there was a lot of lightning and thunder. To drown out the noise, the musicians played much louder and encouraged the audience to clap and stamp their feet to the music. Everyone was yelling 'HEY' when given a signal and the crowd was going as wild as the dancers. Medina's mother was in a circle and everyone was spinning and twirling and dancing about the stage with their partners.

The thunder and rain pummeled the tent. Rivulets of water began running along the inside stands making the dirt floor muddy-looking and mushy. Over and over the claps of thunder jolted the crowd who were now paying closer attention to the water which began to leak onto their heads. A few got up to leave but where could one go in such a storm.

Suddenly a jagged streak of lightning caught the center pole and scurried across to the electrical connections and the tent burst into flames.

There was a mad scramble as people raced for the exits, trampling each other as they piled up at the flaps. Medina was screaming like everyone else but she couldn't seem to get close to her mother who had been struck down by the poles along with some other dancers. The lights went out and the rain poured in. There was panic everywhere as the flames fought the rain and dissolved the tent in its wake.

Medina was holding her mother's tambourine and all she could remember was being swept up into a man's arms and carried outdoors. She cried for hours as she was lost in a crowd of people who had piled into a big truck and were making a muddy escape out of the circus area. Medina was only four years old and she wanted her Mommy.

The following day the newspapers ran stories of the tragedy and there were many people who were dead or critically injured. Medina never heard from her parents again.

Medina grew up in an American household always wondering why she never saw her mother or father again. The people who raised her were her new parents and she loved them as they loved her. But, she never forgot her beautiful mother with the silky, black hair who danced in her beautiful costumes. Medina was content but she was not happy.

Over time she recalled her mother's face with clarity but her other memories faded away with the years. She had trouble trying to piece together this ongoing enigma.

Medina became a social worker and moved to another city where she shared a house with her friends. She got a job in a nursing home and loved helping the families of the patients who came to visit their family members. Medina was a case worker and she gained favor with the staff because of her beautiful attitude and eagerness to help everyone.

One day a new patient was admitted to the facility and Medina went over her chart checking her medical history. The poor woman was not able to recall any of her past due to amnesia. Everyday was a new day to her and everyone she met was like a new acquaintance. The patient was disagreeable and she made life hell for everyone around her.

Medina went to see the woman and upon entering her room, she felt only sadness for the pitiful sight that greeted her. Fragile, white-haired and worn out, the patient called Lydia looked at Medina with an emotionless gaze. Medina spoke with her but trying to make any sense of Lydia's situation was challenging and disconcerting. This was going to be a true test of her endurance skills and she threw her coping mechanism into full throttle.

Medina had no better luck communicating with Lydia for several days and knew if she were to have any success with Lydia, it would be pure coincidence. Lydia was incoherent and distracted. She fidgeted and often turned away to gaze out the window.

Months after coming to the retirement facility, Lydia was taken into the smallish lecture hall where a movie was going be shown that afternoon. It was about a small town in Europe and like most movie showings, some of the patients promptly fell asleep in the comfort of the darkness.

All at once a country scene showed some people gathered around a campfire and a man was playing an accordion and a young woman was dancing with a tambourine.

Lydia yelled out, "That's my Valdir. That's my Valdir."

She began to bounce up and down in her chair, waving her arms and clapping her hands. Everyone began yelling for Lydia to hush up but she continued shouting.

"I know him. It's my husband, Valdir. I have to find him. I want to see him."

Medina rushed to her side and wheeled Lydia out of the lecture hall to her room.

Her heart was racing. What was Lydia talking about? Who was this woman and who was Valdir? She had many questions now and she didn't know quite where to begin.

"Lydia, please tell me, how do you know Valdir? Have you seen him before? It was only a movie, you know. What did it mean to you, dear? You can tell me."

Lydia was very animated now. She began to speak hurriedly as if trying to grasp every word before she lost it.

"Valdir is my husband. He was with me when we played and danced together. He went away from me and I don't know where he went. Can you find him for me?" Medina's heart was bursting in her chest. No, she thought. This can't be what I think. I have not known my mother. This woman could be anyone. Why am I thinking these thoughts?

"Lydia, what dancing did you do with your husband? Can you remember and tell me? Perhaps we can find Valdir together. I'll try to help you find him right now."

Lydia began to cry. It was as if a floodgate suddenly opened. Lydia talked on and on about many things. She spoke of the road shows and the time of the circus. Up to that point she could recall only a few things, then everything was a blank. She began to cry.

"I had a baby once. She was a beautiful child, but I can't remember much."

Medina began asking many questions, trying hard to get Lydia to recall her past.

Lydia suddenly dropped into silence and that was the abrupt end to their conversation. Medina felt frustrated but excited. She left work early that afternoon.

Back at her house, Medina rummaged through some old mementos and under an old pile of junk she came across a fractured tambourine, one with a repaired cymbal.

The next morning she brought the tambourine to Lydia's room and accidentally, if not deliberately, placed in on the table before Lydia, who grabbed the tambourine and clutched it to her bosom.

"Where did you get this? This is my tambourine. I must have left it somewhere."

Tears welled up in Medina's eyes. Gently, she took Lydia's hand in hers.

"Lydia, what can you tell me about that little daughter? Did she look like this?"

Taking a photo of herself as a small child in front of her step-parents' home, she showed it to Lydia, whose eyes brightened and then she began to cry.

"That's her. That's my baby girl. Did you find that in my drawer? I must have left it there. I forget where I put things lately. I wish I could see Valdir again. Why doesn't he come to visit me? Can we go to see him? I'll put on a nice dress and you can take me to him." She smoothed her hair with her hands.

"I'll get my wedding ring and he'll know we're married and I still love him."

"Yes," said Medina, "we'll go to find Valdir and you will even find your little girl. You are going to be very happy when you meet her. She remembers you well."

Over the months that followed, Medina's slight recollections of her mother dancing brought back some memories for Lydia and her treatments began to show promise of memory recall. Newspaper clippings about the fire brought tears to Lydia's eyes. She only remembered up to the part of the tent catching fire. The falling poles injured her and she had a memory loss for several years. Now the doors to her past were opening and Lydia was responding excellently to past regression therapy given in a noted psychiatric hospital.

A few years later Medina and her mother, Lydia, were living together trying to piece together the remnants of their lost years.

Miracles happen if you believe they do. This is just one story about a miracle.

* * * *

Lydia Boroshenko is enjoying a functional life with the assistance of her living facility. She cannot teach belly dancing but, now and then, she entertains her friends with her gyrations. There are no veils or snakes but she can shake, rattle and roll with her little gypsy tambourine.

GOLDEN SLIPPERS

ABIGAIL (ABBY) WEST

FROM THE TIME she was only fourteen, Abby wanted to be grown-up. She would sneak in her room and put on lipstick and put her hair up and walk around in my high-heeled shoes. I didn't make too much of it because it's what young girls do but, when she'd come to the dinner table drenched in my perfume, I knew I had to say something.

"Abby, you smell like a funeral parlor. And what's that on your eyes?"

"Oh, Mom, I want to be as pretty as you when I grow up."

Well, if that wasn't a snow job. (Flattery will get you anywhere.) I had to smile as she would flutter her lashes and walk around the room, stopping now and then to strike a pose. I had to admit, she was a pretty girl who could be a possible knockout someday.

Abby wasn't much for drab colors or plain-Jane clothes so, as soon as she was old enough to get a part time job after school, she went to work at the library to earn extra money for clothes. The library was open everyday and I might add, it was a place for her to make new friends.. Abby wasn't shy about the truth that she preferred boys.

When she was barely eighteen, she met a young man she had a crush on. His name was Joe and he was an exchange student from Ireland.

Joe asked Abby to go to the wedding of a family friend so Abby bought herself a new dress. It was a gold dress with very fine stripes both matte and shiny and it had a full skirt. I imagined it would look very glamorous when she swirled around the dance floor.

Joe went shopping with her and he surprised Abby with a pair of beautiful, shiny gold sling-backs with lucite across the toes and high heels. Very classy, I thought.

Whether it was the music, the dress or the shoes, Joe and Abby found romance that night and they decided they wanted to date steadily. When Abby came home, she woke me to tell me about their decision and then proceeded to extrapolate on every little detail of the night's gala. Listening to her I was reminiscing my own first romance so I could see the stars were in her eyes from that night on.

Abby wore her golden slippers over and over again. When they became worn, she tissued them in a shoe box and lovingly placed them in her closet. Now and then I'd see her take them out and she'd tell me the story of her romantic evening with Joe on that very special date.

Joe and Abby were married and had two children, both boys. She'd always wanted a little girl so she could give her the golden slippers one day but that was not to be.

As the years went by, Abby would rearrange her closet and replace clothes but the golden slippers always remained. They were such a special part of her love and marriage to Joe. Abby was a dreamer and whenever she looked at the shoes, she got a faraway look in her eyes. I thought her keeping the shoes was such a tender gesture of her love for Joe.

Thirty-six years later and the last time that we saw her in her hospital bed, she asked Joe to put the golden slippers on her feet so she could dance her way into Heaven.

And so it was.

* * * *

Vivian West likes to spend time on her computer corresponding with friends and playing computer games. She also likes to knit afghans for the local nursing home where she is a volunteer caregiver. (Her daughter, Abby, was laid to rest wearing her golden slippers.)

SECTION THREE

* * * *

Spirituality

ROBIN
PAULINE ROBINSON BUSH

"So I am glad — not that my loved one has gone —
But that the Earth she laughed and lived upon was my earth, too.
That I had closely known and loved her and that my love I'd shown.
Tears over her departure?
Nay — a smile —
that I had walked with her a little while."
—Author Unknown

When Former President George Bush's mother died in 1992, his letter was given to Former First Lady Barbara Bush as a memento. It was written several years after Robin's death and George's mother had saved it all those years. Little Robin's body was donated to research.

The Brite Star Foundation for leukemia research is named in Robin's honor.

Her body lies in happy repose in Greenwich*, Connecticut. Her soul is with the angels.

Dear Mum,

I have jotted down some words about a subject dear to your heart and mine. It is fun to fool around and try in one form or another to express thoughts that suddenly come up from way down deep in one's heart. Last night I went out on the town and on my way home–late–I said to myself, "You could well have gone to

Greenwich tonight....this thought struck me out of the blue, but I felt no real sense of negligence. The part I like is to think of Robin as though she were a part, a living part, of our vital and energetic and wonderful family of men and Bar. (Barbara)*

Bar and I wonder how long this will go on. We hope we will feel this genuine closeness when we are 83 and 82. Wouldn't it be exciting at that age to have a beautiful 3-1/2-year-old daughter...she doesn't grow up. Now she's Neil's age. Soon she'll be Marvin's–and beyond that she'll be all alone, but with us, a vital living pleasurable part of our day-to-day life. I sometimes wonder whether it is fair to our boys and to our friends to "fly-high" that portrait of Robin which I love so much; but here selfishness takes over because every time I sit at our table with just our candlelight, I somehow can't help but glance at this picture you gave us and enjoy a renewed physical sensation of closeness to a loved one.

This letter...is kind of like a confessional...between you and me, a mother and her little boy – not now so little, but just as close only when we are older, we hesitate to talk from our hearts quite as much.

There is about our house a need. The running, pulsating restlessness of the four boys as they struggle to learn and grow; their athletic chests and arms and legs; their happy noises as the world embraces them... all this wonder needs a counterpart. We need some starched crisp frocks to go with all our torn-kneed blue jeans and helmets. We need some soft blond hair to offset those crew cuts. We need a doll house to stand firm against our forts and rackets and thousand baseball cards. We need a cut-out star to play alone while the others battle to see who's "family champ." We even need someone....who could sing the descant to "Alouette," while outside they scramble to catch the elusive ball aimed ever roofward, but usually thudding against the screens.

We need a legitimate Christmas angel–one who doesn't have cuffs beneath the dress.

We need someone who's afraid of frogs.

We need someone to cry when I get mad–not argue.

We need a little one who can kiss without leaving egg or jam or gum.

We need a girl.

We had one once–she'd fight and cry and play and make her way just like the rest. But there was about her a certain softness.

She was patient–her hugs were just a little less wiggly.

Like them, she'd climb in to sleep with me, but somehow she'd fit.

She didn't boot and flip and wake me up with pug nose and mischievous eyes a challenging quarter-inch from my sleeping face.

No–she'd stand beside our bed till I felt her there. Silently and comfortably, she'd put those precious, fragrant locks against my chest and fall asleep.

Her peace made me feel strong, and so very important.

"My Daddy" had a caress, a certain ownership which touched a slightly different spot then the "Hi Dad" I love so much.

But she is still with us. We need her and yet we have her. We can't touch her, and yet we can feel her.

We hope she'll stay in our house for a long, long time.

Love, Pop

* * * *

Former First Lady Barbara Bush says about her life:

> *"Certainly it has never been boring.*
>
> *George Bush and I have been the two luckiest people in the world, and when all the dust is settled and all the crowds are gone, the things that matter are faith, family and friends. We have been inordinately blessed, and we know that."*

Text taken from her book: *Barbara Bush: A Memoir*

SWAMP ANGEL

MARCY SYDELL

IF EVER A TOMBOY WAS BORN, it was Marcy Sydell. In a Jewish household like the Sydell's, there would be no tomboys. Only dainty little girls with starched pinafores and hair ribbons to match. Her vocabulary included 'please' and 'thank you' with anything she would ask for. You had to pay a visit to Bubbie's house at least once a week and grow up in Momma's kitchen to learn the foods and wines for traditional holidays and religious celebrations.

"So, what's this I hear, you want to become a botanist? That's crazy. You can't meet an eligible doctor or lawyer in the woods. Listen to your Momma because she knows what's best for her little girl. You think we're paying for modeling and acting lessons so you can go into the woods? To model for who, some crocodile?" Momma would laugh.

It took years trying to convince Marcy's parents of her dream for a scientific career but nothing ever worked. They'd talk about giving her a fancy wedding when she was in love; they suggested sending her to Europe for the summertime in the hope she'd come back with a change of heart. They even threatened to take her out of her father's will (well almost). Marcy stuck to her guns. It was botany or bust.

In her senior year of college in another state, Marcy and some of her classmates signed up to spend the month of July in the Amazon on a jungle expedition. Hearing this, Marcy's mother feigned a heart attack but since she refused to have an ambulance take her to the Emergency Room, Marcy knew the theatrics were all for show.

The group of twenty students were put into four teams of five and each team had a teacher as a guide. Marcy was certain this was going to be the most exciting experience of her life. Her chances of meeting a doctor here were about as remote as kissing an anaconda serpent. She giggled at the thought of kissing a snake's forked tongue. It couldn't be any worse than kissing Larry Feinman who always tried to suck out her tonsils whenever he kissed her. She shuddered at the thought and she was happy to know she was far away enough that Larry couldn't get within a thousand miles of her.

The journey was long and everyone was wiped out after putting up a campsite and getting settled in their tents. They had another day of stocking supplies, then they were off to test their guts in the most outrageous trek one could conjure up in a moment of utter madness. Everyone was excited at the prospect of making front-page fame once they got home with their exciting tales and possibly some rare plants and specimens.

The trekkies were on the trail by daybreak and Marcy was grateful for the insect repellent they doused themselves with as the steamy fauna produced insects she had never even heard of. They took occasional photos of wild birds and took notes on their tape recorders. Marcy envisioned herself one day on the cover of National Geographic under a blaring headline that mentioned her name which, by that time, the entire world would be aware of. Here and there they stopped to rest, usually when they came upon something worthy of discussion or after digging their way out of the soggy terrain.

The professor stopped beside a strange-looking "mushroom" thing that clung to a tree. He explained its origin and rarity while everyone listened, noted and clicked off shots with their cameras. Here began the first of a series of newsworthy photos. This thing looked much like a gigantic mushroom but it was greenish in color and it had large bumps on it, the kind that look like a toad's back. Upon closer examination, the professor decided it could be lethal. On the other hand, it might also contain natural properties which could prove valuable to science. He marked the spot and said they'd come back for it on their return. They proceeded to penetrate deeper into the area which was so dense by now, they could hardly see sunlight.

Crossing through tiny rivulets they continued marking their path with iridescent tapes that could be seen at a distance so they would have no trouble locating their "finds" when they headed home again. Marcy felt she was learning more on this trip than she had during the entire year from her book studies. Here she was in a mysterious wonderland where almost no man had ever set foot. She thought of the first astronauts to set foot on the moon and she compared herself to them in some small way. Well, why shouldn't she?

Marcy wanted to retrieve the green mushroom on the way back but the professor thought it had some menacing components and he decided it was not such a good idea. Marcy found herself pouting like a little child when she couldn't have her way. Oh well, she thought, there are bound to be other discoveries in the days ahead.

Later that night, Macy couldn't sleep. She kept thinking about the green mushroom and she couldn't shake it out of her head. She tossed and turned and finally decided she was going back to get it and wouldn't everyone be surprised the next morning?

Dressing very quietly in the dark, Marcy gathered a flashlight and some supplies and tiptoed out of the tent and made her way toward the swamp where the trophy mushroom waited for her. She carefully picked her way along just as they had done earlier that day and she felt very surefooted as she made her way along the trail. She looked for the iridescent ties that would take her to the mushroom and then, back to the campsite.

The night was surprisingly cool in spite of the dampness and the moon sprinkled its light now and then through the treetops. An occasional nightbird called and she even saw some strange-looking owl-type birds peering at her through the inky darkness.

Nearly forty minutes into her walk, Marcy came upon the green mushroom. Taking her insulated gloves and a sharp knife, she cut around the mushroom, carefully extracting part of the root system so she could study it back at the laboratory. Her professor would be so proud of her, she thought. Marcy placed the huge mushroom in an insulated bag and put it into her backpack and turned to make her way back via the trail she had come on.

One, two tapes now. Yes, this is the right way. Three, four.....oops. Where is tape number five? It was here just a few minutes ago. Marcy took a few steps to the left. Nothing. Then she came back and took a few steps to the right. Again, nothing. They were here when I started out, they have to be here now. She flashed her light all around. There were no tapes that she could see. Marcy took a breath and counted to ten. She moved forward a few yards and peered into the darkness. No tapes. She went back a few yards. Nothing as far as she could see. How could this be? she thought. They were all here and there's no one here but me.

She looked up at the moon but the moon was hidden now behind some misty clouds so she couldn't see anything. She didn't bring her compass as they had used the iridescent tapes to mark the path that day. Well, I'll try to wait until dawn, then they can come for me. What could possibly have happened to those darn tapes? They were all here when we came out today. (Yesterday. It was now nearly 4 a.m.)

Suddenly, out of nowhere, a swooshing sound was above her head. Looking up into the darkness, Marcy strained her eyes to see. A large figure thumped down on the ground about thirty feet in front of her. Flashing her light toward it, Marcy let out a little scream as she came face to face with a large monkey. He began to jump up and down with glee. In his hand he held about eight or nine of the iridescent tapes that had marked the path. Marcy choked a sob as she realized what went wrong.

Marcy's mind began to race as she thought of the consequences of her inconsequences. This could turn out to be the worse nightmare of her existence. How would she explain her excuse when she was told specifically by her professor they would not be going back to claim the exotic mushroom. Now she felt like a big, disobedient brat. The thought of her picture on a magazine cover would more appropriately be MAD. Oh, how she was hating this foolish prank. She would be an embarrassment to the group and her classmates wouldn't be wrong if they shunned her in the future. It was all so unnecessary and foolhardy.

Marcy figured she had best make a smarter decision than to sit down and cry. She tried to go in the direction she presumed was the trail she had taken but in reality, she was heading deeper into the swamp on a course that was totally foreign to her as of now. She came to a tiny stream and bent to drink. She stopped. Something told her it wasn't the right thing to do. She was feeling very parched, sweaty and nervous. Her body ached from tension and she was overtired from lack of rest and adequate sleep. Tears came freely. Panic finds its way into the most controlled situations. Marcy felt her chest tighten, her shoulder muscles ached and her legs had grown very weary.

She didn't know what to do to coax the monkey toward her. She might get him to drop the tapes. So what? What would she have done with them anyhow? Next she realized the monkey might spring on her if he thought she were trying to attack him.

One outburst from him might bring an entire tribe of monkeys and that might create a vicious confrontation that could lead to serious injury and possibly...death.

Lightly she tried to shoo the monkey away but he wouldn't move. He smirked as if to mock her. It was as if he knew he had something she wanted and he wasn't about to part with it. Marcy looked away as if to ignore him hoping he'd go away. She wondered if that would only serve to provoke him and perhaps he'd attack her from behind. She didn't know how to conduct herself. She pointed the flashlight right into his face and he covered his eyes. She stood her ground. It was a battle of wits. Then, without a sound, he turned and disappeared into the jungle taking the tapes with him. Marcy didn't know if that meant he was gone for good; worse yet, would he come back with an army of monkeys? Oh, why didn't she just stay where she belonged?

Marcy began to move cautiously but she really had no idea where she was headed. It was still quite dark. In a few hours her classmates would be up and about and they'd miss her at once. Perhaps they'd come looking for her or radio for a rescue team.

Marcy took a few steps and at once she realized she'd stepped into a mud stream. It was very silky, like quicksand. Instantly she was up to her knees in the murky syrup. She pulled herself out and her boots and socks were covered with the thick gooey stuff. It was hard to walk but she didn't want to take her boots off for fear she wouldn't get them back on again. Frustration overcame her and she sat down and cried. She prayed and, for the first time in years, she heard herself saying, "Dear God, please help me, help me."

Looking out into the darkness Marcy saw a glimmer of light. At first she thought of her classmates coming out to her. She called out but there was no response. Wait, there it was again. A very pale wavering cloud of light was making its way toward her. She was fixed on the image but she was too frightened to move or cry out. Who was it? What was it? The image drew closer. Marcy didn't know if she was happy to see it or not.

She squinted her eyes but she couldn't make out what the image represented. It seemed to be floating in the darkness. She couldn't help staring at the cloud that was ever so slowly making its path in her direction. She crouched down as if not to be seen.

Oh, God, please help me. I'm lost and I don't know what to do. I'm also very scared, she thought to herself. Her mind went on. I haven't felt like this since my first roller coaster ride in Disney World's Space Mountain. The image kept floating toward her.

Marcy wanted to call out but her throat was frozen in fear. The image seemed to be taking shape now. It was still hovering above the ground but it looked like the figure of...no, it can't be. That's silly and stupid, Marcy thought. This is not a cartoon, after all. If someone could read her mind, she thought, she'd be immersed in lunacy and taken away. But, if my memory serves me, I'd say that "thing" looks something like an angel. Whoops. There's that word, she thought. My mother would hang me if ever she heard me say that. She didn't believe in angels. The only symbols we recognize have nothing to do with supernatural beings. Closer and closer it drifted before her. It was larger now and Marcy felt it had a definite shape. Well, I'll be darned, if that doesn't look like some kind of an angel.

But, what would an angel be doing out here? Better still, what would it be doing looking for little Marcy Sydell in the middle of nowhere? Why wasn't he...she...it tending to some other business rather than wasting time out here looking for li'l ole me?

Marcy called out. "Hello, is anyone there?" That sounded dumb, she thought, but then, how do you speak to an angel? She tried again.

"Excuse me, I'm Marcy Sydell. I lost my way and I'm out of iridescent tapes and... The professor's not going to like this one bit. My boots are full of some sticky stuff and... Who are you? Why don't you let me see you? How did you get here? Are you lost, too?"

Marcy was hysterically crying and talking in a shrill voice, hands trembling and not making much sense. She felt ridiculous but, at this point, who cared? The image wavered before her and swung slightly to the right.

Marcy's eyes followed and then the angel drifted in front of her again. Marcy watched in amazement. Then the angel swung to the right again, hovered there and slowly came back in front of Marcy's eyes. It was as though it were pointing the direction to her.

Marcy moved forward very slowly, uncertain if she were doing the right thing.

The image moved to the right again so Marcy hastened to get closer.

"Don't leave me. Please, don't leave me. If you're what I think you are, then maybe you can understand what's going on. I'm all mixed up and I don't believe in angels and my mother would kill me if she thought I was praying to an angel, of all things, er, people, whatever."

Now they were both moving in the same direction, Marcy following closely as the image floated before her. It was much bigger now and at one point, Marcy wondered if she saw the outline of a face. Oh, I'm going nuts, I know it, she thought. I'm dreaming this. If I tell this to anyone, they'll put me away. I'll need psychiatric evaluation and they'll put me away. Goodness, I'm talking to myself. I'm talking to an angel, I think. I'm going out of my head and I'm hallucinating, she thought. But Marcy continued to walk toward the image of the floating angel that moved before her on a constant path.

The encounter endured for more than half an hour and Marcy thought she saw a glimmer of daylight overhead. The sky was now a slightly lighter blue and she was afraid if the dawn broke, she'd lose the image which moved before her.

"Please, please, don't go. Don't leave me just yet. Can you get me back to camp? I don't know who you are but I need help. Please don't leave me." It stopped. The angel stopped moving and hovered in place. Marcy stopped walking.

"Thank you, thank you. I know you must think I'm crazy but I don't believe in angels so I don't know what to say to you. You understand. I don't know why you're trying to help me and I can't tell my family I'm a convert so if that's what this is all about, then maybe you just better leave me here until a rescue team comes for me. I'm sorry."

The angel moved very slowly and Marcy remained quiet. She followed without another word. The angel wove in and out of the jungle as if to make a path for Marcy. The sky was getting a little brighter now. Suddenly the angel stopped in front of a tree. Marcy looked at the tree and for the first time, she saw an iridescent tape on the trunk. The angel had led her back to the exact path where the trees were marked with tapes. Marcy began to cry again.

"Oh, thank you, thank you, my friend. I don't know what to call you but you are surely my friend. I don't know what to say. How do I thank you? Who can I tell?"

Marcy began to follow the tapes that showed themselves on the trees. When she looked toward the moving image, it was already moving away from her and dissolving in the morning mist. Another hundred yards and Marcy found herself near the campsite.

It was just a short distance away and as she neared the site, her classmates called out to her.

They wondered where she'd gone and what was all that mud in her boots? Marcy was so ashamed and relieved. She flopped down and she didn't quite know how to explain what she had experienced. Drawing out the green mushroom from her backpack, she opened the zipper bag. The mushroom was wet and very mushy. It hadn't retained its shape and it was smelly and oozing water. The professor took the bag and discarded it. Now she wouldn't even have evidence of her discovery. Marcy was both relieved and filled with self-disgust that she had disobeyed orders. She needed a reprimand and it was well-deserved, she thought.

Abashed by her behavior, she reluctantly told her story to her classmates. She apologized for her misgivings and told how she had seen a vision who led her to safety.

Everyone listened with interest but Marcy could not be sure whether or not they believed her. She was mortified but very certain the image that saved her life was an angel, indeed.

That night, Marcy laid awake trying to think of some way to put her thoughts into words. She wanted to write an essay for her college paper. What would it say? Would she tell of her green mushroom experience or her encounter with an angel, one of which she didn't even believe in? She was in a quandary.

During the years that followed, Marcy told other people about her visionary image and how it saved her life. Would they believe her? Should they believe her?

What did she care and what did it matter. Marcy knew in her heart that her meeting with the Swamp Angel was a true message from God and she would believe it for the rest of her life. On her bedroom wall is a painting of a girl in a swamp with a messenger from God.

* * * *

Harriet Sydell is an Angel Parent who believes the Swamp Angel preceded her darling daughter, Marcy, and took her to a better place of eternal rest.

MIRACLE ON LOAN

JOHN PAUL HENDERSON

BY THE TIME JOHN PAUL got to the first grade he wanted to go live with Jesus. He did not likc living here on earth. Whenever I recalled his remarks I relived the night I lost him, not once but five times. He didn't mean to hurt us with his words; they just slipped out because he had memories of how nice it had been when he was visiting with his friend, Jesus.

John Paul was born on December 21, 1954 in Winter Haven, Florida. In December of 1955 both our boys became ill. The doctor treated them for the flu. My oldest son, Winn, recovered but the baby, John Paul, got steadily worse after his medicine was discontinued.

By January 21 he started vomiting and had constant diarrhea. The doctor advised me to put him back on his medications. I tried to follow his instructions but John Paul couldn't keep the medicine down. His condition got worse and, after several medical consultations by phone, I rushed him to the hospital.

At first John Paul was put in a room with many other babies, but at my insistence, he was moved to a larger private room. This proved to be crucial because he had to have an oxygen tent over his bed and space for the doctors to work.

Between noon and 9 p.m. that night a total of six doctors were around John Paul's bed. One doctor told us that John Paul had died five times; and that, if he were to live, he would be completely brain damaged. He had hemorrhaged from his nose and his mouth.

The doctors had inserted a tube into the outer side of his right foot to give him a blood transfusion.

Everyone was praying for him; even the doctor went to the chapel to pray. I was allowed to stay in the hospital room. I kept my hands underneath the oxygen tent, without talking to my sweet child who was lying there helpless and isolated from his mother's arms.

I was alone in John Paul's room for five minutes when there was a quiet knock on the door. I presumed it was the nurse who asked if I'd mind having someone come in to offer intercessory prayers. She said the person would not look at the baby or me and she wouldn't move about the room. I asked where she would get her. She replied, "We keep her upstairs." I said,"Yes, it would be okay."

A minute later a rocking chair was brought into the room with a short woman who had black hair or wearing a black cap which covered her head and ears. She and the rocking chair were just inches away from the opposite side of John Paul's bed. The woman made no sound but she rocked back and forth never looking at my son or me. She was facing the double window.

All the time, I continued to pray my selfish prayer to God telling Him why He shouldn't take my baby away from me. I reminded God of all the good things I had done for Him and I told Him I would continue to do them. But, God was still taking my child.

At 4 a.m. I looked down through the oxygen tent and I saw John Paul's lifeless little body with closed eyes. His face and skin had turned a deep, dark brownish color.

At that moment I began praying for God to do with my little son whatever He knew was best. I didn't know if I could take care of him even if he lived. I vowed that whatever He willed for my child, I would continue to love and serve Him and I would raise my other son to love, obey and serve Him for the rest of his life.

Within minutes of offering this new prayer to God, strange things began to happen. The room was dark except for the tiny light over the lavatory some feet from the head of the bed. At the far end of the room a thick fog was entering through the large double window. It drifted all the way across the room over John Paul's bed. As it passed over us it wet my arms and neck and covered the little light over the lavatory. Then, just as it came into the room, it drifted away from us and vanished through the window.

Suddenly I was stunned by the brightest light I had ever seen coming through the same double window. It was so intensely bright, I had to close my eyes. I could feel the light as it moved slowly over my head toward the door behind me. Then, like the fog, the light passed back over me toward the window. As soon as it passed over John Paul's bed and through the window, I looked down and my beautiful John Paul was awake smiling. His eyes were open and moving. His skin had returned to a beautiful light natural color. The woman and the rocking chair were gone.

Quickly I summoned my husband, Pat, and we ran down the hall calling for the nurses to come see what had taken place. A nurse came in every half hour and dropped a little Coca Cola on the baby's tongue. He would drink it and smile.

Around noontime on Sunday, after God had brought John Paul back to life, he pulled himself up and stood up, holding onto the bed frame. Then he jumped up and down smiling so happily.

Surely we had been visited by God Himself. The Winter Haven Hospital listed John Paul's recovery as a 'witnessed miracle.' They called my son Miracle John.

I had to wait two years before a doctor would examine John and tell me what had caused the severe illness. A specimen from his spine showed the illness to be encephalitis of the brain which had been caused by a bite from a mosquito that had bitten a horse. We lived in an area of citrus trees and a pasture with several horses.

When John reached the age of three, I took him to a brain specialist in Tampa, Florida. The results the doctor gave me made the miracle even more amazing. He told us there was no brain damage. The only thing wrong with his brain was he couldn't hear the long and short vowels correctly. Astonishingly he had a high IQ.

John Paul had a very sweet disposition and he made friends easily. He must have had some recollection of his illness because, from the time he got to the first grade until he left this earth, he kept wanting to go and live with Jesus. He said over and over that he didn't like living down here on earth. Memories of the miracle remind me just how special and precious John Paul was.

After the Christmas holidays in 1978, we never knew we were hugging our son for the very last time. Though he lived a short life, he touched a lot of people. John was a wonderful son and we miss him; but, we also know that now he is living peacefully with his friend, Jesus, whom he loved so much. His presence in our lives was truly a gift from God who gave us a miracle on loan.

* * * *

Lillian June Rudd Henderson was born in 1921. She graduated from Florida State University (BA) and from University of Florida (MA) and taught in Florida Public schools for 35 years. She is married to Pat Henderson and had two sons, John Paul and Winn. Lillian is a member of the Southern Baptist Church.

TAD'S NECKLACE

ROBERT THADDEUS "TAD" ELLSMORE

"WITH A NAME like 'Thaddeus', who'd wanna play with me anyhow?"

Tad Ellsmore hated his name more than he hated eating carrots. He said they both gave him a bellyache and a lot of gas. (I'd say that was reason enough, wouldn't you?)

When you come from a line of Thaddeuses and you weren't lucky enough to be born a girl, you were stuck with it. His mom always assured him, when he grew up, it wouldn't mean very much in the big picture. Tad wondered how long THAT would take.

He was your average American kid, middle class, second generation Irish/English/Welsh. His father told him they were descendants from a long line of bluebloods.

Without much money Tad figured the whole thing wasn't worth a tinker's damn. Nevertheless, his father insisted he sign his full name with a Roman numeral V. Most people didn't know what it stood for and Tad always had to explain that he was the fifth generation and that the V wasn't meant to be another name added on. It always got so darn confusing, he just figured it wasn't worth the time it took to explain.

It didn't mean a thing to Tad while he was in junior and senior high. He was a nice kid with good manners, good grades and made the college entrance exams.

He wasn't afraid of much but on the other hand, he wasn't one to take reckless dares. He drifted into the background or just hung on the fringes of conversation not to look completely stupid. Now and then he'd throw in his two cents from the peanut gallery. In all fairness, I think Tad underestimated his abilities. After all, he was a star on the college swim team and he played a good game of golf, something his cronies didn't.

He wasn't bad-looking and he said he swam because he felt sure the pool's chlorine helped get rid of his acne so it added a little benefit to the splash.

Getting through college was no tougher for him than most but Tad grew into a role he didn't know he was about to play.

One year he decided to save money to attend a special seminar to learn more about his spirituality. He felt this might help answer some of the questions he had about the eternal journey of life after life. We didn't have enough money to go on the parents' tour so we stayed home. Tad saved his portion and we told him we'd be content to hear all about it on his return. We let him keep part of the summer job money he paid for board at home to help pay for this trip. Just the name made me tingle for it sounded so exotic — Tanganyika.

The small group of college adventurers gathered in the airport for the endless flight to Africa. Everyone was in a highly excited state of expectation, including Tad, which was unusual for him. He was usually very reserved, self-contained you might say.

He made a decision to stay up for nearly forty-eight hours prior to departure so he would be able to sleep through most of the tiresome flight. It was a good choice.

Droning over the globe the plane seemed like a little speck in the vastness of the heavens. By the time dawn broke above the clouds, Tad was ready for adventure.

Once on the Dark Continent, the group met their guides who transported them over a trek of interesting terrains, through tribal villages and farms, over endless stretches of nothingness until the dust was so thick, they had to hose down the windows.

Arriving at their destination, rooms in the little barrack-type building had no windows or doors and everyone unpacked to prepare for their first day of initiations.

Early the next morning the pack was up and ready for whatever substituted for the usual bacon-egg-n' cheese on the run. Looked like they were going to be getting used to some pretttty rare-looking mush, a far cry from dunkin' donuts and a cup of joe.

In lieu of his usual after-shave, Tad sprayed on a walloping dose of mosquito spray and joined the others in the outdoor "classroom".

Wow! I heard wood was plentiful here but there are no desks, he thought. This was a very different class, classroom and teaching agenda for these rookies. It didn't take long before they learned to get their own meals, wash their own dishes and clothes, build and maintain a campfire which was used for nearly everything, and sleep on a thin straw mattress and pillow.

I worked all summer for this? I could've had a new car, he thought.

Everyday was supposed to get easier once you got used to it. Yet, everyday got a bit harder because there was always something they weren't expecting. There wasn't a phone within a hundred miles. You never went to a store. Supplies and food were sent in every week. You took whatever you could get and exchanged the things you didn't want with the other students.

Quickly the guys learned to catch fish, scale, cook and eat them whether you liked it or not. They mixed everything with coconut so the taste wasn't so bad. The coconut milk was constipating but then so were carrots. He liked the coconut milk more.

Tad didn't want to be left out of anything and he determined himself to do whatever it took to overcome his shortcomings and face his demons with manliness.

The big test came for him when the weekend event was going to be a celebration in honor of the tribal head of their neighboring village.

Everyone was invited to attend a special dinner and ceremonial rites affair. With all the anticipation of a visit from Santa Claus, Tad prepped his camera for the killer photos he would bring home and talk about over the whole next semester.

Much to Tad's amazement and relief, the dinner was a roasted wild pig. For a while he was fearful they'd be invited to eat some disgusting insects or vipers or monkey brains fresh out of the skull of some still-screaming ape. The thought made him heave.

The meal wasn't so bad once he saw the pig roasting over a bed of hot coals. With it was served some fruit like apples, potatoes and gourds. They drank wine which had a very dizzying effect and it tasted a little bitter. He wondered if they put some potion-type mix in the wood chalices they drank from. Tad knew it would be very bad manners to opt for water so he went along with the program.

When the meal was over, hands began clapping and strange music came from the surrounding trees. In the firelight they could see tribal members emerging from the bushes in body paint and headdresses. Most carried spears and wore skimpy thongs.

There was tribal dancing and more drinking, heads and bodies spinning to the beating of drums and little flute instruments. The entire scene became mesmerizing.

Earlier someone threw more coals on the fire and the redness hissed as a bit of water forced the steam to escape. Tad could feel the heat's intensity on his face.

Now it was time. The chief and Tad's village leader stood together as he announced that all brave warriors got their manhood by walking over the burning coals. It was unheard of to refuse. Tad panicked at the thought that refusing might mean cowardice and that was surely punishable by the noblest end, death.

Nobody wanted to be the one to walk on the burning coals and Tad could see the tribal leader looking very displeased as he felt it was a sign of disrespect.

Tad didn't want to wait to see what might happen. Something told him they would not be harmed because they were here as students on a friendly educational journey.

In an effort to convince the students that this was an honorable thing to do, one by one the tribal members calmly poised themselves at the edge of the burning bed of coals.

Without hesitation they calmly walked across the coals as cheers went up over the crowd. None of the students budged an inch or took a breath. Everyone was entranced.

Whether or not it was the wine or the deep-seated fear, it didn't matter. No one moved.

Tad was feeling like he wanted to run away, be home, be anywhere but right here, right now. His entire body was in a sweat and he was shaking all over. As he recalled, this was not in the brochure or their chosen itinerary.

"Oh, God, do we really have to do this? Sweet Jesus, what're we gonna do now? I've never been a martyr and I'm not about to volunteer now. Please, give me a sign."

The steady beating of the drums went on as if waiting for someone to take the lead.

Tad was certain his heart was beating just as loudly but darn it, he wasn't the least bit ashamed. No, he was plain scared! He shut his eyes real tight as if hoping for a sign, a vision, anything. He opened them. Nothing. It's as if everyone was frozen in place.

He unclenched his fists. To his great surprise, his palms were dry. A sudden calm came over him. He felt composed, serene. His eyes caught the tribal leader's. It was time.

He stood up very slowly. All eyes turned in his direction. Across the darkness, he could see the eyes of the tribal leader burning into his own. In the glint of firelight, Tad looked from right to left without moving his head to see where he might go.

Hah! That's a good one. Where to go? Nowhere, stupid. You're here and this is it.

It's either the beginning of something...or the end of something. He wasn't sure which.

His heart was still pounding. He wondered if they'd let him die quickly or slowly so he could feel the pain searing through his body as his blood flowed on the ground.

He'd been called a fool before but never over something like this. Imagine how his mother would feel when they sent his body home without honor. Maybe they should just put him in a pot of boiling water and eat him! Oh, that wine sure is scaring the piss out of me now, he thought. I worked like a dog to come here for THIS!? He wanted to crumble.

The tribal chief's eyes were still gazing intently into Tad's. He didn't dare look away. He had to do something. He couldn't just stand here forever. It's getting old now.

Slowly, slowly Tad made his way over to the coal bed. He stopped just at the edge and very slowly lifted his arms up to the sky. Without warning, a shrill piercing scream came from his throat and he held it like a 16-beat note. His arms fell to his sides.

He unbuttoned his shirt and threw it to the ground. He turned his eyes upward.

Tad sucked in his breath and put his arms out before him. In the next moment which seemed like an eternity, he stepped onto the coals and put one foot in front of the other.

A hush came over everything. Even the wind and leaves stopped rustling. Not a breath was drawn or expelled. The only thing that moved was the changing glimmer of lights from the burning coals.

Tad never lowered his eyes. He looked straight ahead as if in a trance. Step by delicate step he made his way over the hotbed of embers. In a few seconds he stepped off the far end and paused. His arms lowered. His head lowered as if he wanted to know if his feet were burned. The quiet was like a film strip that had stopped running.

All at once a great cry went up into the air. The spell was broken. The tribal leader and his soldiers ran to Tad and embraced him, smiling and lifting him high on their bare shoulders. They took him to a clearing and began to sing and dance holding him high in the air. Now everyone was smiling and happy. They began to laugh and nod their heads as a sign of great approval. This went on for several minutes. Then they took him to the tribal leader and gently set him down on his feet.

The leader took Tad's foot and lifted it. There were no burns. Then he rubbed oil on them and stood up. He took Tad by the shoulders and smiled widely. He took a very ornate necklace from his neck and placed it over Tad's head as a sign of honor. Then he motioned for Tad to sit beside him. There was simultaneous applause and everyone began to walk over the coals following Tad's performance. It was a night of sheer splendor.

Tad took his little camera and flashed some photos and the tribal leader was all smiles revealing a very white set of large teeth and a huge saber tooth taken from a tiger.

The experience was earth-shaking for Tad. It changed his life forever. From it he learned that his true strengths came from the depth and height of his spirituality. His ability to believe that the spirit that lived within him enabled him to do great things.

He was capable of doing things that he would never have dreamed. Dreams that allowed him to fulfill his life's desires far beyond the imaginable.

Tad always believed from that day on that tapping into the wellspring of our inner strengths rewards us with the untapped treasures of our lives.

* * * *

Mrs. Leticia Ellsmore's favorite photo of Tad shows him wearing the necklace given to him by the African tribal leader for his outstanding courage and spiritual belief.

CRACKED

MAARTIN WARSHINSKI

EVER NOTICE how the smallest thing can become a formidable obstacle if it's in your pathway to success? On the other hand, it's been said that faith can move mountains.

A habit can be the most difficult thing to change once it has hold of you. We develop habits because they are the easy road taken. Its convenience bears a high price.

The strongest man is like a mosquito in the face of a bad habit. He doesn't have it; it has him! A man with a habit is as weak as a kitten, has the attention span of a gnat and the patience of a snowflake. Maartin Warshinski's habit nearly killed him.

One day he smoked so many cigarettes, his heart nearly stopped cold. He couldn't breathe anymore. He couldn't walk much anymore. Everything he ate was tasteless.

Like so many smokers before him, Maartin tried to quit. He went to every program, tried every patch, isolated himself and nearly jumped from a high bridge. He failed.

One day he fell on his knees and cried. Strange stuff for a man with no religion. He begged God to help him. He wanted someone, something to take away his cravings. He knew if he didn't change his life very soon, he'd have no life to change. It was that simple. Maartin was never much for praying. He only believed in himself. Lately that wasn't saying very much. He was just thirty-seven and he didn't want to die.

He took a week off and went into seclusion. He needed time to think about this. Perhaps he should sign himself into a hospital or a program for addictions. He was a blue collar worker so he didn't have a bushel of money to spend on rehabilitative care.

Sitting quietly in his room one day, he heard himself speaking aloud to no one there.

"If I can get rid of my smoking habit, I promise I will preach to other smokers."

The promise was simple and direct. He said it over and over to himself, then he slept. That night he dreamed he saw an angel standing on a pile of boulders. The angel was a young man about his own age. In his hand he held some seeds.

The scene was unfamiliar to Maartin. When he awoke he felt as if he had seen that pile of boulders somewhere in his past. He searched his memory for that place.

That weekend Maartin went to the country where he thought he may have seen such rocks at one time. Sure enough, they were near a cliff. When he looked over the edge of the cliff, he thought he saw the image of a man who had fallen and was dead. Upon closer examination, he realized the man was himself. The image disturbed him greatly.

Maartin went home and was shaking uncontrollably. How did he happen to go to that place and what was the message of the image he had seen? He needed to know.

That night he prayed again vowing he would forego his smoking habit. When he went to sleep, he dreamed he saw the angel who stood on the boulders. This time the angel tossed a seed onto the rocks. Maartin awoke in a sweat. What did the message mean?

Several weeks later, Maartin swore he would break his habit or die trying. He left his job, which was very important to him. He stayed at home and did little else other than pray for the angel to appear to him once more so that he could understand. The angel did not appear so Maartin went back to the place where he had seen the boulders.

He had tried to stop smoking as he had become desperate from fear of dying. He did not go out for fear of wanting to buy cigarettes. He kept very busy in his house. He did not have contact with other people. He kept praying for the angel to give him a sign.

The weeks dragged by. Maartin did not smoke but he felt like a nervous wreck. He tried to keep very busy so he took up woodcarving to keep his hands busy at all times. He made a few decent carvings and sold them at a local outdoor flea market.

During the months that followed, Maartin had become rather prolific with his woodworking. He was beginning to conquer his habit because he kept his hands and mind very busy. Nearly a year later, Maartin awoke one day without craving a cigarette.

He got through the entire first day without a desire to smoke. That night he had a dream about the angel. The next day Maartin drove out to the boulders.

He stared for a long time at the place where he had envisioned the angel. He also looked over the cliff almost fearful of seeing his image at the bottom of the cliff. There was no image anywhere. He got ready to leave the spot. As he turned to go, he caught sight of the large boulder with a dark jagged line running through it. He went closer to it and when he stood almost on top of it, he saw that it was a huge crack and in the crack was a tiny stem with a tiny bud on top. It was exactly where the angel in his dream tossed the seed.

The following week Maartin returned to the boulder. There was a pretty little flower in full bloom growing out of the boulder's crack. He stooped to pick the flower but something stopped him. Maartin turned and went home. He had a sign from the angel.

That night he dreamed of the angel. He said to Maartin,

"You have been a rock of strength. You planted a seed of determination and out of the rock, the seed flourished with promise. Your resolution has been your reward. You are the flower that broke through the rock. You have earned your true reward."

Maartin made his life a career teaching smokers to quit as he promised he would.

Maartin never smoked another cigarette as long as he lived. He was the angel.

* * * *

Maartin's father, **Edmond Warshinski**, lives in the mid-west where he owns a small shop that sells hand-carved figurines. Mr. Warshinski has never smoked.

SECTION FIVE

* * * *

Loyalty

CAN THERE BE TOO MUCH LOYALTY?

MICHAEL KANOFSKY

WHOEVER SAID A DOG is man's best friend made the understatement of the eons.

When Mike was a baby we bought a German Shepherd to keep him company, be his friend and mind our store. It was just a little dry goods store but when the little place around the corner was robbed more than once, we felt it was time to get a guard dog.

My doctor told me there wouldn't be any more kids for us. Mike was all we had and we felt a dog would have taken the place of a little brother or sister. You can look at it that way or this way: You might fight with your brother or sister but your dog will stand by you and love you even if you threw him off a rooftop. For all you dog lovers, you know what I'm saying. Every man's dog is the world's best dog, period.

As a toddler, Mike would ride around on Nero's back and the dog would allow himself to be led around by the scruff of his neck by his beloved little master. The two were inseparable and Nero fell into his role as Keeper of The Child.

He became the father figure while little Mikey was learning to walk and talk. He knew everything Mikey said to him. Nero responded to Mikey's baby talk commands and I often wondered if the Almighty didn't install a comprehensive mechanism between babies and pets.

Life was Utopia for the two until the day we took Mikey to kindergarten. Nero just didn't understand and accept the fact Mikey couldn't be at home all day to play with him.

Nero spent the entire first day by the glass door watching for Mikey's figure to come into view. He wouldn't leave the door long enough even to eat so I thought it was time to put his bowl next to the door if he was to get some nourishment or water. It was difficult for Nero to understand why Mikey suddenly had to leave him for hours on end. He wasn't being punished; he simply couldn't understand.

Summertime was Nero's favorite time. Mike was out of school and they were both growing up and doing "big guy" things like hiking, swimming and riding around in Grandpa's truck as he made his deliveries. On very hot summer days, Mike would reel out the garden hose and he and Nero would play and splash on the Slip 'n' Slide.

By nighttime the two were thoroughly exhausted and they'd fall asleep on Mike's double bed. With a dog the size of Nero, a single bed was out of the question.

On Grandpa's little farm Mike and Nero would romp around acting silly. Mike would hide and Nero would have to find him. Of course, they pretended it was a big mystery but Nero always found Mike and Mike always told him what a smart dog he was.

Nero was very proud to please Mike and he spent a lot of time showering Mike with doggie kisses. I doubt there is any greater love than a dog for its master and vice versa.

One day Mike's attempt to rescue a small kitten up in a tree was his undoing. He climbed up to dislodge the kitten and somehow missed his footing. He plummeted to the ground, breaking his leg in two places and gashing his head and arm on the sidewalk. He was knocked out cold. After getting no response from Mike, Nero came to the door and barked furiously to let us know something was seriously wrong.

The ambulance arrived. The paramedics scurried around doing things to Mike that Nero wasn't familiar with. Something like this had never happened to Nero and suddenly he felt like an outcast. Mike was not awake so there was no assurance for Nero.

As Mike was whisked away on a stretcher, Nero was very dismayed that he couldn't ride in the ambulance and that he was forced to remain at home. Poor Nero. Nobody was paying any attention to him. He was feeling very sad.

It was terrible to see his reaction.He seemed helpless and very confused. We tried to comfort him but he was growing old now and he did not have much patience for learning new things. This was one thing he simply didn't wish to accept. He made it plain by his attitude that he felt very disturbed by the major disruption in his association with his pal Mike.

At the hospital, Mike was in surgery to reset his leg and repair his bruises. With his head in bandages and leg in traction, it would be at least ten days before he would be home.

On returning home from the hospital there was little attention paid to Nero as Mike's condition was the topic of conversation at the dinner table. Nero refused to eat and he went directly to the spot where Mike fell. On the ground was a huge blood stain.

Nero laid down over the stain and cried for the longest time. We tried to coax him into the house but Nero refused to budge. His beloved Mike was not here and his blood meant everything to Nero. By dusk, I had to bring food and water outside as Nero refused to come into the house.

By the time it got very dark, we went outdoors to find Nero. He was still laying over the blood stain which was now dried on concrete and turned dark. As we approached Nero, we spoke gently to him, trying to reassure him that Mike was going to be alright.

It didn't mean a thing to Nero. All he knew was that Mike wasn't there and he was not about to move from that blood stain until his beloved master came to get him.

Once again, I brought Nero's food and water outdoors so he would eat and drink. Near midnight my husband took a walk outside to find Nero and coax him into the house.

Nero would have none of it. He looked up with the saddest eyes in the world. Apparently nothing was going to move him from that spot until Mike was home again. We did everything possible to convince Nero that Mike would return. Then my husband tried to pick up this monstrous animal who was now slumped down like a limp rag doll.

Nero resisted any attempts to go indoors and at one point he growled at us to let us know he wasn't going anywhere, PERIOD!

During the night we looked outside and we called to Nero. He would raise his head, lower it and stay there. Our attempts were futile. Nobody got any sleep that night.

Early the next morning we went to the hospital to visit Mike and check his progress. He was awake and having some pain. The first question he asked was, "How's Nero taking it?" We explained what happened and Mike began to cry. Twelve years old and a sad dog brought more tears to his eyes than the pain to his leg and his skull. It was written.

The routine continued for another whole day. Nero was refusing to eat now and spent the entire day crying and whining as he laid over the blood stain on the sidewalk.

We took turns trying to comfort Nero but the sadness was rapidly taking its toll on the old boy. He was thinning out and looking very pitiful. It made us cry to see him.

I wondered, how could an animal allow himself to just wither away like that? Was he never going to eat or drink again? How long could this possibly go on? I speculated.

Nero was wasting away and the grief was catching up with him. I began to think he was going to die. The thought of it broke my heart. I knew if anything happened to Nero, Mike would be devastated. I begged Pete to do something or we would lose Nero for sure.

By the fourth day my husband bought a can a paint and, pushing Nero aside, he painted the sidewalk gray where the blood stain had left its indelible mark. It was as if he had scorned Nero's loyalty. Nero was entirely insulted as my husband placed a huge galvanized tub over the freshly-painted stain. Nero tried to push the tub away and he sat down beside it as if to try to figure it out. Quickly he flopped down on the sidewalk and cried and whined for an endless period of time. Soon it became howling and more howling.

Pete and I were totally perplexed. How long and how far would Nero take this role? Pete went to the phone and called the hospital. In a few minutes he threw on a zip-up jacket and headed out the door, slamming it as he went. Within a few minutes I saw him pick up Nero and load him into Grandpa's pick-up truck. He beeped the horn out front and grabbing a sweater, I ran out and jumped into the seat beside him.

At the hospital we took Nero as close to the window of Mike's room. The nurses had opened the window and Mike was there, waving with his good arm and calling out to Nero. For the first time in days, Nero jumped up and down as if trying to reach Mike.

His powerful tail nearly whistled in the wind as he cracked it back and forth with joy at the sight of his beloved Mike. Nero's voice was rough and dry but he wouldn't stop barking as he let Mike know how much he had missed him and to please tell him that he'd be coming home soon to play with him again. Remarkably Nero threw himself into the air over and over in an eager attempt to tell Mike how much he loved and missed him.

"Nero, Nero, Nero. I'm here, boy. I'll be home soon. Good boy, Nero. Good boy!"

We spent about ten minutes waving to Mike and watching him and Nero having their little reunion. It was a poignant, beautiful sight. I couldn't hold back my tears as I experienced this overwhelming show of love between two hearts beating as one. No vocabulary but there was a clear understanding now. Upon returning home Nero wouldn't leave the sidewalk but he ate and drank now.

Early the next two days Pete took Nero back to the hospital. Nero caught on immediately. He jumped into the truck as soon as Pete got in the driver's seat. By this time Mike was in a wheelchair and downstairs at the entrance. Nero nearly killed him as he lunged onto Mike's lap nearly breaking his leg all over again. There were more tears, a lot of barking and many hugs and doggie kisses. Mike wouldn't need to wash his face for a week.

Mike seemed to improve greatly and Nero's health was no longer a threat. He now came indoors after visiting with Mike and he spent most of the day lying on their bed quietly ticking away the hours 'til he would share the bed with his best friend, Mike.

A few years later Mike and Nero were laid to rest side-by-side as the result of a crash in the little pick-up truck. Nero had been riding in the back and was thrown out. He had been fatally wounded by an oncoming vehicle which could not stop in time.

It probably was exactly how Mike and Nero would have wanted it.

* * * *

Peter and **Marge Kanofsky** are semi-retired living in Pennsylvania.

SECTION FIVE

* * * *

Tickling the Funny Bone

CRIME AND PUNISHMENT IN THE PLAYROOM

ANTHONY WAYNE STOCKMAN

TONY WAS NEARLY two years older than Tim and they were different as night and day. Just four, Tony was an easygoing child, sweet and mild-mannered. Tim came into his terrible two's with excitement, cunning and loads of energy.

At times I wondered if Tony were envious of Tim because he constantly took Tim's toys away. Poor Tim, I thought. One day he might stand up for himself and fight back for his toys. Frequently I scolded Tony and demanded to know why he always felt the need to take Tim's playthings.

"Tony, did you take Tim's toys?" and he'd always say, "Yes, but..."

Well, that was enough for me! I didn't want to hear another word.

"Young man, I don't want to come back into this room one more time and find Tim without his toys, is that clear?" Tony would simply lower those large brown eyes in acquiescence and never utter a word. He knew when he was wrong, or so I thought. I guess it worked for a while because things seemed to right themselves for a spell.

One morning a friend dropped by for coffee. Once we heard a thump thump and a yell, but then it stopped. A little while later and...Whump! There it was again. I couldn't imagine what the neighbor thought so I brushed it off quickly.

"Oh, boys will be boys, you know." She smiled a little and, for a moment, I thought I saw her roll her eyes upward in disbelief. Oh, well, I thought, what does she know about kids anyway? I didn't think much about it and, when my friend left, I fixed lunch and went upstairs to call the boys.

Upon entering their room I was shocked to see Tony sitting in a corner surrounded with an arsenal of toys. He was almost waist-high in the midst of a few Tonka trucks, his baseball bat, some tin soldiers, and his 3' tall stuffed chimpanzee, the one his father won on the boardwalk. There was an army helmet, part of a Leggo building set, his Dad's old baseball glove, one roller skate with only three wheels, and an assortment of junk that came from who-knows-where and were parts of who-knows-what.

Tony was completely absorbed in his self-contained center of the universe, unaware of the fact Tim was sitting the middle of the floor without one single toy, not even the yo-yo without the string.

"What the heck...". I couldn't believe my eyes! Here was my sweet little darling Tim, all by himself, innocently looking at me with that ever-so-special look that always melted my heart. I couldn't help but notice that cute little space where the new tooth was coming in and at times, when he smiled, it looked more like someone had knocked a tooth OUT! My precious innocent angel was being taken advantage of by his overbearing, selfish big brother who had "stolen" every single toy for himself leaving poor little Tim.... Why I just couldn't stand it another minute.

"Tony!" I gasped. "Why are you treating poor Timmy so badly? What has he done to you to deserve this?"

Before Tony could answer I was scooping Tim up in my arms when — I saw it. Good Heavens!

"Tony!" I screamed, " What's happened to Tim?" and Tony responded in his usual soft manner,

"He's okay, Mommy. He just faw down."

"But, he's got two black eyes!" I gushed.

A moment of silence, and in a soft little voice, Tony said,

"Yeah, Mommy, he faw down A LOT."

And from that day on Tim never stole another toy from Tony ANNNNYMORE!

* * * *

Margaret Stockman met her husband, Bill, while they were in the US Navy. Traveling around the United States was fun but it cut into her motherhood time with three little children. Now retired in Gilbertsville, Kentucky. Margaret is a voracious reader and she loves to bargain shop.

WHODUNNIT

MICHAEL IACONIS

FROM THE MOMENT he made a grand entrance weighing in at nine pounds, seven ounces, Michael had three chins, a large round body and he looked like a halfback in training. In spite of the nurses wrapping up his head of dark hair with a ribbon, he was the epitome of an old soul in physical features and personality.

Star Trek was Michael's all time favorite television show back in the 1970's. He'd watch the show religiously. Every night he slept in his homemade uniform made up of red pajamas, complete with feet, black cowboy boots and a sheriff's badge, his version of the *Star Trek* pin. He had to be "beamed up" to bed every night.

Michael loved those pj's so much, he wore them to bed every night until he outgrew them. Those pajamas had to be replaced and washed when he wasn't looking for he rarely let them out of his sight. I think if it were possible, he would have worn them until he was ready for his high school graduation.

Michael had a great imagination. By age three he found a crawl space hidden in the back of his closet where we would hear him whispering and carrying on lengthy conversations. Eventually, Michael told us about his friends who lived in the closet — Rude, Chop, Fiddie and Fire," to name only a few.

Whenever Michael did something naughty and one of us scolded him, that old sweet twinkle in his eye would appear. He would look naively at us and say,

"I didn't do that...Rude did."

You can't blame what you can't see.

* * * *

Joyce Newcomb is a psychologist with her own successful practice in Boca Raton, Florida.

Her husband, Robert, is a successful writer with several books to his credit. They love doing everything together and they enjoy a lively circle of friends. As new grandparents, Joyce and Robert love visiting their grandchildren who live in the northeastern part of the country.

A WHISTLE'S AS GOOD AS A HOWL

AMY ROLLINS

IT ISN'T EVERY DAY YOU GOT TO SPEND three glorious days on a cruise ship when you are just twenty-one. Cruising today isn't what it was some years ago. At that time, only people with money to burn or retirees were privileged to cruise the open seas on a luxury liner. The masses of middle-class travelers were content with less luxurious vacations and something like this only happened in your dreams. Well, for most of us anyhow.

Amy and her best friend, Jennifer, were taking a holiday cruise out of their home city of Fort Lauderdale, Florida, to experience the Western Caribbean and the Bahamas.

The girls were overjoyed at the thought of meeting interesting people and seeing new sights that appeared in windows of travel agencies which boasted faraway places.

Jennifer was wearing a sundress design of fancy seashells in the pattern while Amy chose a sundress of black and white flowers with pink flamingos around the hem. They looked as though they had just stepped out of an ad for *Conde Naste* magazine.

Arriving at their cabin, they unpacked their luggage and Jennifer set up two glasses to prepare a toast to their weekend of great expectations. Oops, the ice bucket was empty.

"Would you go down the hall to the ice machine and fill up the ice bucket?" asked Jennifer. "I'm nearly finished unpacking so I'll mix two cocktails."

Amy gingerly stepped out of the bathroom after reapplying her lipstick. She grabbed the ice bucket and took off down the corridor. The ice machine was situated just around the corner from the Purser's Reception Desk. The new voyagers were still checking in and there was an atmosphere of excitement everywhere.

This is going to be to be the vacation of a lifetime, thought Amy. I hope we get to meet a few nice men we can spend time with and go dancing at night.

Filling up the ice bucket, Amy began to make her way back to her cabin. Just then a long, low whistle rang out. It told her someone had noticed her and was flirting. She held her head a little higher, swung her hips a little harder and threw a quick backward glance in the direction of the whistle. The fun was about to begin. Someone already whistled at her and the outlook was promising.

In their cabin, Amy couldn't wait to tell Jennifer about the guy who whistled at her as she was leaving the ice machine. As Jennifer began to mix the cocktails, Amy blurted, "I can't believe I'm already getting this much attention. This is going to be a great cruise and we're going to have a ball."

She took the drink and twirled happily around the room. Jennifer burst out laughing and said, "I'll say you're drawing attention. Just turn around and look in the mirror. You'll see why you're such an attention-getter."

Amy swung around and her face turned beet red. Her skirt was hiked up into her panty hose and her bikini panties were a sight for sore eyes.

Amy spent the entire weekend wearing a large sunhat and dark glasses. This was a cruise she would never, ever forget.

* * * *

Amy's parents, **Rick Rollins** and his wife, **Joanna**, feel this story launched Amy's cruise life with a hilarious backlash. It became a fond family joke once Amy outgrew her embarrassment.

OVER EASY

TOMMY LOGAN

"THOMAS JONATHAN LOGAN, if I have to tell you once more to stop this nonsense and be still until you're through with breakfast, you'll rue the day you were born!"

Tommy knew when his Mom called him Thomas Jonathan she meant business.

You know those days when you get the laughing fits and everything strikes you so funny, you just can't stop? When you laugh even if you know you're likely to catch the dickens but you do it anyhow? Well, it was just that kind of day and in the pit of his stomach, Thomas Jonathan Logan knew there would be a price to pay. Come what may, he didn't care. He was having too much fun.

"Aw, Mom, c'mon, if I listened to you every time you said I'd rue the day I was born, then there wouldn't be too many days left!"

Tommy burst out laughing over that one and he was just doubling up in his chair. Maybe I should go back to the very beginning.

It was raining cats and dogs that morning. Dad was already late for work because he had a head cold that wouldn't quit and he was just all stuffed up and coughing and sneezing and wheezing till I thought he'd collapse.

Marcy had soiled her diapers and she must have caught a bug because she threw up in her bed and she was screaming for Mom to come and get her. Mom just rolled her eyes up, brushed back her unruly curly hair and mumbled under her breath, angry at Dad for not being much help. But when Dad was sick, he was as much work as Marcy on a bad day.

I'm Patty to Mom, Tricia to Dad and Patricia Ann Logan when Mom had it with me. I guess we all have our days and Mom was having one of those "PMS" days she tells her girlfriends about. I think it means something like Pretty Miserable Syndrome.

Anyhow, Tommy was no help whatsoever and Mom was about ready to explode.

Dad was just sitting there, feeling as bad as he looked. I think he was going to work just not to have to stay home and listen to Mom's litany of "it was nothin' like she read about in those True Romance magazines." She was still waiting for the house with the picket fence, not to mention the fairy tale Ozzie-and-Harriet-family that went with it in her dreams.

"OKAY, OKAY, I'm coming, Marcy! Just hold on a bit. Patty, please go and take care of your sister."

"I can't, Mom. I'll miss the bus and it's raining too hard. I just can't," I said.

Mom kept on scrambling the eggs and putting in the toast and burning the ham.

"Geez, Mom, why do we always have to have scrambled eggs, all runny and slimy? Why can't we have "over easy" or french toast or pancakes like Frankie's mom makes?"

Tommy was really pushing now. Mom had one last nerve left and he was standing on it.

"Because Frankie's mom doesn't have a helpless army like I have here," Mom came back sarcastically. I kinda felt a little sorry for her at that moment. It was all stacked up against her that day, for sure. I figured I just better not add to her misery.

Just then Marcy came into the kitchen with her diaper around her knees, stinking to high Heaven and wailing at the top of her lungs. I ran to her and got her to the powder room before Mom would have a stroke.

All of this was just too much for Tommy and he laughed so hysterically, I almost had to laugh, too. It was like a scene in a movie. TV was tame by comparison.

Tommy was holding his stomach and rocking back and forth in his chair. He just couldn't get over the giggles. Just at that moment Mom was coming closer to the table with the platter of scrambled eggs and ham when it happened.

Tommy threw his head back laughing so hard, he hit the platter and the whole thing went upside down on his head. Scrambled eggs and ham were all over him, down his shirt and on his lap. It all happened so suddenly, everything STOPPED cold!

Tommy was so stunned, he couldn't speak. Dad's eyes opened so wide. All you could hear was his wheezing. Marcy and I just stood in the doorway, spellbound. Mom froze in her spot. There were two or three seconds of complete silence while it all registered.

Then we were all laughing at once. Everyone but Tommy, that is. He was covered with scrambled eggs everywhere. The laughter was deafening. It broke the ice.

Only Cappy, our dog, was too busy to notice. He was having breakfast fit for a king, er, pedigree. I think he ate more eggs that morning than he had in his entire life.

The best part came when Dad dropped off Tommy at school and he had to tell his teacher why he was late. Come to think of it, I don't believe Tommy ever ate eggs again.

* * * *

Patricia Logan wrote this story for her mother who has a slight memory loss. However, this is a story about Tommy she has never forgotten and we doubt she ever will.

TO AN IRISH JIG

SAMMY McHENRIE

OUR LOCAL ELEMENTARY, JUNIOR AND SENIOR high schools had an annual Spring Festival which featured various choral groups, dance numbers and others entertainment. There were tumbling and juggling teams from the high school, tap and ballet from the junior high school and little ethnic dance groups and skits from the elementary school.

Everyone turned out to support their children and the schools they attended. There were also money prizes for the various types of numbers which included some elegant trophies. The participating students took great pride in appearing on stage and everyone exhibited great showmanship in an effort to be team Number One.

Auditions for singers, dancers and jugglers began in the fall and tryouts for the tumbling teams were held shortly after the new year began. Gym instructors, music teachers and parents got together many hours after school each week to coach, encourage and hone the skills of these dedicated youngsters.

We were a family with a proud Irish heritage. It was very exciting when our son, Sammy, came home and told us he was chosen to be part of a dance team. He was going to dance in the Irish segment of the show much like a precision chorus line.

Actually, it came as no surprise to me because my mother and I were crazy about dancing. Before she became too old to dance, she would often take the children's hands and show them how to dance the Irish jig in the old world tradition. It was a lot of fun to watch her lift her skirt and dance on her tip-toes in the old style of her Irish parents.

Mother would grab Sammy's little hands from the time that he could walk and they would dance around the house, especially when he was acting cranky. Within a few minutes she would get him laughing and dancing with her and having a grand old time.

Sammy loved his Grandma very much and he literally grew up dancing.

My mother could no longer dance as she did when she was younger but she always enjoyed watching Sammy practice his steps for the chorus line which was much like the Riverdances we enjoy on television today. They are reminiscent of the dances of her past.

After many months of practicing, Sammy was having difficulty with one particular routine and somehow he just didn't keep pace with the other dancers. There were a few steps that puzzled him and he responded poorly during that routine. We kept up our applause for him and told him he'd be as good as the others on opening night.

Months went by and the night of the Spring Festival finally arrived. The school grounds were jammed with cars and people were streaming into the auditorium in droves.

I tried to arrive a little earlier so I could take my mother to her seat down front. She wanted to be close to the stage so she could see her beloved Sammy and keep time to the music with her feet.

Back in the dressing-room, Sammy was munching on a small box of cookies which he always said gave him energy before the show. The dance teachers were all excited as there were many new numbers to enthrall the audience and they were very proud of their dancers and soloists.

Meanwhile Sammy went into a locker room to review the steps that had troubled him lately. When the lights began flashing, he returned to his dressing-room to get ready for the overture which would signal the on-stage cues.

In his knee-high black stockings, Sammy pulled on his knickers, tucked in his peasant shirt, slipped into his dance shoes and took his place on stage with the others.

The lights were low as everyone got into position. Then the music notified the audience that the famous Irish jig was about to commence.

The audience began to clap their hands in time with the music. As the curtain parted, the colorful lights lit up the stage to reveal a spectacular outdoor scene with a backdrop that represented a hillside country setting.

The dancers moved in precision with one another to the pulsing tempo of the jig. They moved accurately to the left and right in an excellent pattern of perfection.

Now it was Sammy's turn to dance his solo portion. He danced with all his might as we'd never seen him dance before. His feet pounded out the rhythm and his face was rigid as he stared straight ahead into the darkness of the audience. Faster and faster he moved, slapping his hands at his thighs and kicking his feet and pounding harder and harder in time with the music.

Soon he was slapping his buttocks and whirling and twirling around. He was all over the stage. The audience thundered their applause and by the time Sammy was done, the people were on their feet. Sammy took a quick bow and ran off the stage. The curtain came down and quickly went up to honor the dancers. Everyone but Sammy was on stage.

The curtain came down for a second time and then went up again. More cheers. No Sammy. I looked at my Mother in a questioning manner but we didn't say anything.

We waited for Sammy to appear. Soon the applause died down. Out on the stage came the dance instructor. He raised his hands to maintain quiet and everyone waited for him to speak.

"Ladies and gentlemen, thank you so very much for your show of appreciation to our fine dancers. The show isn't over but we won't be able to get Mr. McHenrie out to accept your applause at this moment. However, let me assure you, he is fine and we will continue with our next number, if you will. Maestro, if you please..."

When all the numbers were over, the curtain went down for the final time and everyone began to leave the auditorium. The performers had taken all their bows and the night ended on a lively note. There was a great deal of buzzing with favorable comments for the show and the hard work that went into making it the success it was, surpassing the previous years. It was a show that would be talked about for the entire school year.

The next day everyone could be pictured sitting with their morning coffee reading the local reviews of this popular annual event that made us very proud of our students.

A small article caught my eye which spoke about Sammy's notable performance. It was clear to see why Sammy danced as never before. The headline read:

"Ants in his pants keeps dancer on his toes" Mother and I broke into peals of laughter. It seems the cookies from the night before were so appreciated by the ants that filled Sammy's britches, they helped him do an Irish jig the world would not soon forget.

* * * *

Nancy McHenrie's Mother never lived long enough to see this story about her grandson's accomplished dance recital. It made her happy to know Sammy learned a lot from her early teachings of the Irish jig. We can still laugh about this story as we remember him.

ALL YOU CAN EAT? SO WHY AM I HUNGRY?

GIACOMO (JIMMY) CORDINO

WHEN I FIRST CAME TO AMERICA many years ago, I was so impressed to see that my son, Jimmy, was able to get dressed in a three-piece suit and go out to fancy restaurants.

You see, where I came from, we never had much money. I could count on one hand the times I went somewhere fancy. Maybe it's not polite to say this but, if it weren't for weddings, christenings and funerals, we never got to go anyplace where the food was free.

My husband died at a very young age so I was a widow most of my young life. I wanted my son to have better opportunities than to grow up in a little town. I ironed clothes for some local families and I saved every lira to pay for Jimmy's ticket to America.

If he only knew how many times I didn't eat for the entire day just so I could put an extra little bit away in my apron to give to him someday. But, when you do it for your son, you don't feel the pains of hunger so much. That's what a mother does for her children. Then it's no sacrifice.

It took several years for Jimmy to save enough money to bring me to America and I promised the Lord that I would do everything I could never to be a burden to him. When he wrote me that I would be leaving our little town within another year, I cried the whole time for happiness. It was all I could think of; it was all I could speak of.

Just think, my Jimmy would be sending a ticket for his Momma to come to America.

As poor as we were, I felt very rich whenever I told that story to someone. They say time flies; that year was like holding my breath for twenty years. Finally the day arrived and I made the flight to New York like a prima-donna. I didn't sleep one wink. Somehow I couldn't seem to get enough to eat so I asked for seconds of everything. To look at my thin little body I think the stewardess knew I could use the food.

To my great surprise my son took me to his apartment by car, HIS car. All I could think of was that he must have secretly married a very rich woman, held up a bank, or won some kind of lottery. It was almost impossible for me to comprehend that my son earned so much money at his job that his refrigerator was always full and we could eat and watch television at the same time. Oh, Mother of Mercy, I've died and gone to Heaven!

One day soon after I arrived, Jimmy took me to a beauty parlor and then he bought me a new dress, a pair of beautiful suede shoes and a genuine leather purse. He said we'd be going out that evening to a beautiful, expensive restaurant and he even bought me a pair of gold earrings. The only piece of decent jewelry I ever owned was my little band of gold which I received on the day I was married. God Bless that wonderful son! From that time on I knew my life in America would be an everlasting blessing of God's love.

I promised myself I would try very hard to learn to speak English so I could understand and appreciate being in this country. I wanted Jimmy to be very proud of me.

We went to a beautiful American restaurant but I couldn't read the menu so he ordered for me. Here was the most succulent and tender steak I had ever seen in my entire life and it was all on my plate. There were three vegetables, a salad and a side order of crisp golden onion rings. We even had a special bottle of wine on the table.

I didn't want to appear too hungry so I barely tasted the food. I filled up on one or two rolls with butter and sipped on my wine. Jimmy asked me if I didn't like the food and I assured him it was quite delicious. Little did he know I could have licked the dish for how excellent it tasted. The fragrant aromas made my mouth water.

He beckoned to the waiter and spoke quietly to him and the waiter shook his head understandingly. Very soon he came to our table with another plate of food, this time two pork chops with another variety of vegetables and some greens and beans. Once again I took a few tiny bites and said that I didn't want to eat anymore. Jimmy looked at me and he seemed puzzled. I didn't want to upset him, of course.

Once more he called the waiter who took away my plate and Jimmy sounded like he was a little annoyed but he was trying to be patient with me and I appreciated his good manners.

Now the waiter approached and he, too, looked a bit disgruntled. This time he had some wonderful roast chicken and again, a variety of vegetables and a potato.

Before I picked up my fork, Jimmy said, "Momma, I hope you will enjoy this chicken. You didn't seem to want the other dishes I ordered for you but please, try to eat something. If not, I will ask the waiter to wrap it up and we'll take it home. I don't mean to bring this up to you but this is a very expensive restaurant and everything I've ordered must be paid for. All this food is being wasted and you haven't eaten a thing. I know you must be hungry for we've been shopping all day and you hardly had anything to eat since your morning coffee and toast, so please, Momma, eat something!"

I could not believe my ears. I was trying so hard to please my son and he was accusing me of being wasteful. How could he think such a thing? I began to cry.

"Oh, Jimmy, I have enjoyed everything so much but I didn't know you had to pay for whatever you DON'T eat. I thought I could sample a bit and then you wouldn't have to pay so much money for all the food. I didn't want to cost you a fortune on our first night out."

"Oh, Momma, this isn't like it was years ago in the old country. Whatever you order is what you pay for! I have to pay for every entree I ordered."

Well, I can tell you now that I ate every morsel of that chicken, the vegetables, the rolls and butter, the salad and even some dessert! I would have stuffed the leftovers, the rolls and butter and yes, maybe even the tablecloth and napkins. We sat and laughed over it afterwards. My, oh my, did I have a lot to learn! I'll never forget that night. I wanted to die at the thought that all that food could have been mine. How could I ever have passed up such a feast?

This is a story I'll never forget and I have told it hundreds of times over the years.

My son and I laughed every time but since that night, I never went hungry again. Better than that, I never wasted another morsel of food in a restaurant ever again.

As for Jimmy, he never held it against his poor Momma from the old country.

* * * *

Signora Catherine Cordino, 87, is now partially blind. She lives with her niece and her ten-year old cat, Checkers. Mrs Cordino has never returned to her town in northern Italy. She has learned to speak English and she spends most of her time watching TV reruns.

APPLE TREE SURPRISE

CHARLES PETERSEN

MY HUSBAND had the most beautiful apple orchard in the county. We depended on the harvests for our living so any damaging storms could have been a serious detriment to the following year's revenues. Like most harvesters, great care had to be taken until all the crops were delivered and the money was securely deposited in the bank.

It was the life of the apple that sustained us and we knew everything about apples from the seed to the hot pies we served at mealtimes. Strangely enough, as much and as often as we peeled, cooked, baked, preserved and ate apples, we never tired of them.

John was happy to give his big juicy reds to anyone who came his way; however, there was one hard rule he would not tolerate being broken. He had a passionate dislike for anyone who stole his apples for he said they were "taking the food out of our mouths." To him stealing an apple was worth a blast in the pants with his shotgun.

When Charlie was a youngster about ten, he wanted to own a B-B gun to go into the woods with his friends and shoot wild rabbits. My husband, John, didn't object to the idea very much. He had had a B-B gun when he was Charlie's age so he didn't think it could do much harm since rabbits was all they were after.

There was one catch, however. John wanted Charlie to earn his own money for the B-B gun and Charlie wasn't very keen to doing extra jobs around the barn. Charlie had a better idea.

Charlie had a friend named Joe Baxter who owned a B-B gun. They made an agreement that he'd trade Charlie a sackful of apples for the gun. That meant Charlie would have to get the apples from the back of the orchard where John wouldn't see him.

The boys would have to go all the way around the outer fence and pick the apples from several trees so it wouldn't be very noticeable that a lot of apples were missing. Charlie figured when he got the B-B gun from Joe, he'd keep it hidden somewhere and go shoot rabbits with Joe without John finding out about it. (Good planning, Charlie.)

The two boys picked a day and a time when Charlie would steal the apples while Joe stayed on the ground with the empty sack and he'd fill it up as Charlie threw the apples down to him. That way they could be out of there in short time and the deal would be done without a hitch. (Good planning again, Charlie.)

On the appointed day, Charlie climbed the apple tree and one-by-one tossed the ripest apples down to Joe who hurriedly began to fill up the sack. This was going to be a great day for Charlie. There were always going to apples but there was only one B-B gun.

Charlie whacked at the branches to jostle the luscious red fruits and they hardly resisted. These were the biggest beauties that would fill a sack in a hurry.

Suddenly, without warning, Charlie let out a scream. He had whacked into a nest of hornets and they were not the least bit happy about the disturbance. Hornets began to swarm around Charlie stinging him everywhere. Joe began waving his arms dropping the partially-filled sack of apples and he ran down the back road as fast as he could.

Meanwhile, poor Charlie was desperately trying to descend the tree while trying to keep the hornets from stinging his head. Hornets were all over him, stinging him for all they were worth and Charlie knew it. He yelled and yelled but no one heard him.

His face was a perfect target for the hornets and they zoomed in from every angle. Charlie kept yelling and waving his arms. Just then he lost his footing and fell from the tree injuring his leg. The hornets couldn't care less. They were more furious than ever. Their intruder had started something he couldn't finish and they wanted their revenge.

Charlie hit the ground with a hard thud which cost him a broken foot. He fell at least twelve feet but the hornets pursued him. Poor Charlie. He scrambled to get on his feet and let out another scream which came from the bottom of his foot. Now he was in so much pain, he couldn't tell which was greater; his hornet stings or his broken foot.

He cussed under his breath. If only Joe hadn't left the apples in the sack when he ran away, maybe Charlie would have had some alibi for the hornet stings and the broken foot. As it was, he figured when his Dad found out what happened, he was in for another pain, this time on his butt.

Charlie hopped, hobbled, crawled and cried all the way back to the house. He was a sorry sight, if I must say so myself.

The moral of the story: Charlie never got a B-B gun and, as for that coward Joe, Charlie didn't care whether or not he ever saw him again. After a tongue-lashing from his Dad, who secretly thought Charlie had probably already had a good lesson, he laughed whenever we recalled the incident about that fabled B-B gun.

As for Charlie, from that day on he hated apple pies!

* * * *

John and Beth Petersen still maintain their home but the apple orchard is run by their daughter and her husband. Charlie's wife is raising their young son, Charlie, Jr.

FALLING FOR HER IN A BIG WAY

GEORGE DEVERICHE

THROUGHOUT JUNIOR and senior high schools our son, Georgie, was a gymnast. From the time he was a little child he would jump, tumble, roll, flip and somersault He was a born natural so by the time he was able to take gym classes, he was in his glory.

He tried many things but tumbling was his favorite. They are better known as acrobats but he always called himself a "tumbler." He spent most of his youth in sneakers and tights.

His greatest thrill came when he was in high school and his team won the state competition. The young men proudly displayed their photo of the team and their trophy in the main hall of their high school. Georgie kept his on the wall of his bedroom.

Georgie had a secret crush on a girl two years younger. He was a little hesitant to ask her out as he was afraid of rejection, not uncommon in his teenage years.

The state competition was a very big deal to these young men and their trainers. Georgie was very excited when he found out his "crush" was going to be in the first row with her parents. He kept peeking out from the backstage area just to look at her. I must say he had good taste for she was a very pretty girl with a sweet smile to match.

Georgie was in almost all the numbers being performed. He wanted to make a great impression on Vickie so when he did his solo, he threw in a few more jumps and tumbles to wow the audience. Oh, he wowed them alright. He couldn't see the edge of the stage because of the footlights. Tumbling once too often, he went over the edge right into the band shell smashing two music stands and knocking down both musicians.

At first the audience laughed thinking it was part of a comic routine but Georgie was so embarrassed, he quickly recovered and meekly crept offstage. Only then did the audience realize it was a big mistake so they began to applaud thunderously. Georgie was too shaken to take a bow.

He was teased constantly about how he "fell" for Vickie but something good came of it. He got to know Vickie very well and they dated all through their college years and finally married a year after they graduated.

We loved to tell this story of how Georgie fell for Vickie — it changed his life for the better.

* * * *

Georgie's parents, **L. George Deveriche** and **Francine** live in Louisiana. They own and operate a paint company called Brush Strokes Paint and Wallpaper.

GREEN WITH ENVY

SUSAN MACALEAR

SOME GIRLS LIKE TO PLAY WITH DOLLS. Some girls like to play with boys. Susan was a girl who looked like a doll who liked to play with boys. Y'know that kind of cutsie look some girls have like Shirley Temple? The ones with the big round eyes and the curly hair and dimples? Well, that was Susan and she was not the most popular girl in school.

The problem was Susan had a big ego for her age. At thirteen she knew she drew attention and it made the other girls " green with envy." She always managed to get a title role in a school play, voted the Girl Most Likely To Succeed, never got a failing grade....just the kind of girl some girls love to hate!

Every year the local high school held a show entitled "Primavera" — Springtime.

It was a medley of soloists who sang or played instruments, chorale groups, magicians, gymnasts, poets, orators, jugglers and dancers. It ran during the Spring Break week while school was out. Its purpose was to raise money for school projects and new uniforms for members of the band and the sport teams.

This year Susan was appearing in a few dance routines and, much like Broadway shows, there were some tap dance numbers accompanying the soloists. While these young people were not professional dancers, they worked hard practicing their routines under the watchful eyes of their gym teacher who had been a Broadway chorus gal in earlier years.

The costumes were made by mothers of students who volunteered their time each year to help make the event a huge success. This year the costumes were brilliant with sequins and spangles and headpieces which gave the chorus line a professional look.

One of the numbers in the show was a duplication of the famous Gene Kelly hit, "Singin' In The Rain." It was the first time the school had ever done anything of this type and everyone was very excited. There was going to be an entire network of plumbing apparatus set up to create the "rain" which would make it a spectacular number.

Susan was going to dance with a young man and this would be their big scene. Preparing for the number in the dressing-room backstage with the other dancers, Susan was getting into her specially-designed costume for the "Singin" routine. Her costume was a bright Kelly green plastic, hooded raincoat with white plastic boots and a green-and-white see-through umbrella. Very chic.

Just off right stage, Susan listened for her cue. The rain was right on target and the set looked great with little bits of thunder claps and lightning bolts to set the rainy mood.

At the precise moment Susan stepped onto the stage and began her dance routine making her way across the stage to meet her partner. Everything looked great and when she came onstage, the audience broke into applause. Susan was elated as she sang and danced her way through her number.

Then something happened! Unbeknownst to Susan, her costume started to "bleed" and rivulets of green dye began running down her face and legs. Thinking it was part of a comedic scene, the audience began to roar with laughter and applause. Susan kept right on singing and dancing completely unaware of her dilemma. Her blonde hair was turning bright green right before their eyes but Susan just kept on singin' in the rain.

Her partner saw what was happening as the streams of green dye ran down Susan's face. By this time the audience was highly entertained and, upon looking down, Susan saw her legs had "turned" green but she decided to finish her number with style and grace.

She and her partner took their bows, the "rain" stopped and the curtain went up for two curtain calls. The audience was on their feet and by now Susan was laughing, too.

Seeing her face in the dressing-room mirror, Susan didn't know whether to laugh or cry. She didn't want to take herself too seriously so she laughed about the whole incident.

Her sincerity and playful demeanor endeared her to the other girls and from that time on there was a lot less envy between Susan and her school chums.

For the first time they got to see Susan "turning green!"

* * * *

Martha MacAlear was a switchboard telephone operator for a large company in her younger years. Presently she is retired and lives quietly with her two cats, Caspar, an all-white Angora and Jelly Bean, an alley cat.

HAY IS FOR HORSES

ALPHONSE BASCOMB

IOWA IS MOST PRETTY when the grain and corn fields are full and blowing in the breeze. If only more people could see the farms that are rich with the golden harvests and the grazing dairy cows that dot the landscapes, they would know that surely God is nigh.

The girls are the the lovliest of flowers with their creamy skin and dazzling smiles. Five daughters with that kind of beauty is more than any man could ask in richness. My husband was so proud of his girls, he took every opportunity to show them off to anyone who came by the farmhouse. They were as smart and mannerly as they were beautiful. I always knew in my heart that one day we'd be blessed with a dozen or so grandkids just like our own. We also had a son, Alphonse, number two child, named for his proud Grandpa.

My husband, George, was a grain farmer like a lot of men in that part of the country. He took a lot of pride in his land and his crops. He worked hard and our children were trained to grow grain from the time they could crawl. I wanted Alphonse to go to college before taking over the farm and that meant giving up our son for four or five years.

In most families, the son takes over as second man in the house so it wasn't going to be easy for George and myself to handle all the work. Thank Heaven we had good help.

The girls were good at picking up the knitting and baking and I was grateful for their help when we put up all the preserves and meats for the winter. Yes, we were truly blessed.

During the autumn months we looked forward to the holidays because all the crops were in. From the time the pumpkins were ready, the kitchen was always busy with baking homemade fruit pies and late summer berries from which we made our own wine.

One of the things everyone loved best were the summer and fall hayrides. The barn was packed full and George would load up the wagon to join the other farmers and their families on the sing-alongs and the night picnic feasts around tables and campfires.

The summer that Alphonse came home from school was a very new experience for us. He had grown up a lot and he was entering his senior year. He even met a young woman at school and they had been dating most of that year.

We were happy when Alphonse asked if he could bring the young lady home for a weekend so we could all meet her. George made lots of plans to go fishing and hunting but Alphonse wasn't very interested in those things now that he'd found a new flame.

Frances was a city girl who'd never been on a farm and all this was new to her. She was very nice, very citified and very thin. As a vegetarian, she didn't eat much but veggies and a lot of greens. We couldn't entice her to take even a tiny bite of smoked pork or even our leanest cuts of bacon. Forget the butter and real cream. I think she preferred wood chips and fresh tomatoes. Well, I guessed we'd have to get used to each other's ways.

By the third day George was hoping Alphonse would give him a hand with some of the chores but Alphonse only wanted to spend time with Frances. When George complained to me about it, I tried to think back to our courting days which I reminded him of. He grumbled a little bit but that's how fathers are and we mothers need to know it.

Alphonse and Frances disappeared for several hours. By early evening George was getting a little perturbed as we were getting ready for the hayride and we wanted Frances to be a real participant in the farm life we knew so well. However, Alphonse and Frances were nowhere to be found.

George moved the wagon toward the haystack to pile it up before harnessing up our horses. He was trying hard to deal with the fact his only son was ignoring him of late.

The huge pitchfork hissed its way into the haystack as George drew out the hay and tossed it onto the wagon. A couple of pokes and the wagon would have a nice covering on the bottom.

Suddenly a yell went out from the haystack and out jumped Alphonse, rubbing his backside. He and Frances were hiding 'neath the hay and fell asleep in each other's arms.

George was just as surprised and he yelled at the same time, never expecting to find Alphonse in the haystack. Frances emerged sheepishly and a little embarrassed. George broke up laughing at Alphonse as he rubbed his sore behind.

"Well, son, I can't say much about that. I seem to remember a time when my Daddy caught me in the haystack with your Momma. It must be a family tradition."

That night everyone guessed what had transpired when they saw Alphonse limping around and sitting on a soft cushion. It was a giveaway to the others who knew what had been Frances' first farm experience.

* * * *

Anna Bascomb sees her grandchildren when Frances comes to visit the farm. Frances still lives in the city but she will always remember Alphonse, her first summertime love.

BEWARE THE CHIP

DANIEL AMBERCOMBE

Ever since his high school science class did a study on brain mechanics, my son, Danny, became enamored of the body's complex intellectual and reactionary "computer." It helped him make the decision to major in neurological science and he went into it in high gear. He was diligent and eager to try anything that would enhance his career. We were proud of his choice and prayed for his success with great enthusiasm.

In college Danny volunteered to have a microchip installed in his body to record emotional impulses based upon various levels of physical and mental changes. This was part of a study being done for the military to treat men in combat and dire situations.

A high frequency beep would sound in his head to help him control his emotions and think rationally under duress. The chip, placed close to the outer ear, would be removed in six months to gather results of the experiment.

Everything was going well and we were all looking forward to hearing about this great new project which might mean a breakthrough in how troops would be trained in the future. If successful, the program would possibly become useful on the domestic scene.

At home, Danny's fiancee planned an April wedding and a honeymoon in Maui. Everything fell right into place and the wedding went off without a hitch. Well, almost. In Maui Danny and Carol got more out of their honeymoon than they expected. Apparently something jarred the chip and, in response to Danny's excitement level, the chip's high frequency let out a string of short high-pitched beeps during lovemaking. At first, Danny was so shocked, he couldn't calm down long enough for the chip to stop beeping so he had to take a cold shower to chill out. Carol was very understanding and they laughed about it, at first.

However, every time they neared intimacy, the chip let out a frantic series of beeps, each time sounding more like a panic button going off. Time for another shower. By day five Danny spent nearly as much time in the shower as he did in the bedroom.

Danny tried being passive but that wouldn't work when Carol would snuggle up to him. They tried playing it very cool and they approached each other demurely. But, when things started to heat up, that darn chip always seemed to know it and suddenly, beeeep, beeeep, beeeep, beeeep, beeeep in rapid-fire succession.

We never got any details of their romantic nights in Maui and maybe there wasn't very much to tell. As soon as Danny got home, he arranged to have the chip removed. As for the data and the chip's performance? The report read in part:

"Microchip sounds an alarm when engaged. Not recommended during foreplay."

* * * *

Danny's parents, **Dan** and **Marian Ambercombe**, have gotten so much mileage out of this story but it always brings a laugh to everyone who hears it. They share many great memories about Danny and Carol but certainly this is their favorite story.

PIECE O'CAKE

MATHILDA JUREWICZ-GOPFF

My husband and I couldn't figure out where Tilda got her wild personality. Stan was a man of simple tastes, quiet and unassuming. I came from a large family but I was not the one who drew the most attention. We were like a matched set.

Tilda was assertive, daring and a little brash, a total opposite of Stan and myself. No matter how many times we questioned her personality, we couldn't figure it out. She came into the world screaming and it took twenty-four years before we saw a change.

Let's go back to that memorable occasion of her husband's birthday party. Manny and Tilda had been married for nearly two years. Now that she had a nice job, she wanted to do something special for Manny's thirtieth birthday so she planned a surprise party. She invited all Manny's co-workers, his fishing buddies and his parents to a private room in a nice restaurant which served a lovely buffet and an open bar.

She even hired a DJ and a photographer to shoot a video so they could relive the event. You see, Tilda and Manny eloped so they never had a real wedding and she felt this was the next best thing to a big bash celebration. It seemed like a good idea ... at first.

The big night arrived. Manny was duly surprised and impressed, and happy that he was being honored with Tilda's surprise party. Everyone was having a good time. Around 10 p.m. a set of double doors opened and a monstrous cake was wheeled in. Everyone held their breath as the lights were lowered and Manny was going to blow out the candles. The photographer moved in to get the commemorative close-ups.

The drinks were flowing pretty freely and some of the guests were feeling no pain. As the Happy Birthday song ended, the top of the cake opened and up jumped Tilda in a skimpy pink ruffled bikini-type teddy. She threw her arms up in the air and shouted,

"Happy Birthday, Manny!" and as she did so, the bikini top popped open and there she stood before seventy-five pairs of eyes all staring into her 36C's.

At first some people laughed, some gasped and Manny's mother fainted. The Rabbi and his wife got up and left followed closely by Manny's boss and his wife while Tilda grappled with her bra top. Losing her balance, she fell out of the cake and landed on its layers toppling the whole display to the ground.

The photographer kept shooting the scene, the DJ cranked up the music and the crowd was in stitches. My husband ran after the Rabbi and I began to sob.

The few people who were looped thought the whole scene was great but Manny, his brother and I were not appreciating Tilda's idea of a surprise.

If there's a good ending to this story, I guess it was the big change in Tilda. She never lived it down and she never mentioned surprise birthday parties again.

Manny managed to keep his job for a while but the Rabbi and his wife never answered their phone when Manny called.

As for the video, I'm sure the Legion of Decency would have designated it as "CENSORED."

* * * *

Stanislau and **Leandra Jurewicz** live in Wisconsin. They are retired and spend a lot of time raising parakeets and cockatiels which they sell over the Internet. "Birds Of A Feather" is more of a hobby than a business. They take life and themselves less serious these days.

DONUT COP

NILS SCHROEDER

"OH, A WISE GUY, EH?" Nils glanced at the new bumper sticker on his car which read 'No Donut — Bad Cop.' "Verrry funny. Well, it wouldn't be so funny if I wrote him a ticket, would it?"

The car ahead of him turned the corner and Nils was forced to keep on going as he had to be at his precinct in the next ten minutes or miss the briefing. He put on some speed all the while muttering under his breath. His sidekick, Snuff, ignored him and just kept looking out the window. When Nils got his dander up, it was best to keep quiet.

Oddly enough the briefing included an aside where everyone was reminded not to pay much attention to snide remarks, graffiti or bad language when there was a full moon. It kind of made a lot of people do things that they normally wouldn't other times of the month. Some guys were tough and there never was a need to provoke trouble. Like all other police officers, Nils had heard all the bad jokes about cops, all the slang names they were called and anything negative one could think of. It wasn't always easy to roll it off your back but his dad said there was "more than one way to skin a cat." Nils was about to put that philosophy to the test.

Next morning he bought a dozen jelly doughnuts and put them on the seat beside him. One or two was par, thought Snuff, but a dozen seemed a bit much. He eyed the box and then looked at Nils questioningly.

"So, what's with the box of doughnuts? You goin' on a binge, or what? he asked. "You'll need a gallon of coffee to wash those down." He laughed.

Nils lifted his eyebrows and smirked. "Wait'll you see what I'm gonna do with `em. I got a new plan and a new outlook. From now on, I'm gonna be "Mr. Niceguy" to everyone I stop. Wait an' see. If I have to write `em a ticket, they get a doughnut. That way, they'll think twice the next time before breaking the law."

"That's crazy and you're nuts. What makes you think it's gonna change things or change people? They're still gonna roll through stop signs, try to run a red light and drive over the speed limit, you know that!" Snuff was laughing at Nils' foolish reasoning.

Nils didn't respond. He had better ideas.

The day went by unremarkably. It was after 4 pm and Nils had eaten four doughnuts. When it was time to leave, he handed the bag to Snuff to take home to his kids. The next day, sure enough, Nils flagged down a young guy who went through a stop sign and wrote him a ticket. He said, "Hey, Howard, the next time you think about running through a sign, think twice and don't do it, ok? Here, have a jelly doughnut so you'll know that cops are good guys just doin' their job."

The young man was so taken aback, he actually thanked Nils, they shook hands and Nils went back to his car as the fellow drove away.

He said to Snuff, "See, it worked. I knew it might change something."

For the next week Nils kept giving away doughnuts with every ticket he wrote. Each time he got a smile and a kind word and a promise to be a better driver. His plan was working like a charm. Snuff was amazed and they both laughed at the surprised responses they received.

Nearly a year later, Nils was coming from Dunkin' Donuts when an armed bandit ran from the pawn shop a few doors away. He was firing shots at the store as he ran toward a waiting car.

Nils pulled out his revolver and fired a shot as he yelled for the bandit to stop. The man turned his weapon toward Nils as Nils was jumping in front of his parked police car. Nils fired another shot hitting the tire of the getaway car and the bandit returned the fire. Meanwhile Snuff had fired shots at the getaway car and the driver was hit. The bandit was apprehended by Snuff and soon other police cars were on the scene.

The big joke at the precinct came when Nils bit into a doughnut and guess what? In the middle of the jelly was the bandit's bullet which might have been meant for Nils. Nils had the doughnut cut in half and preserved in resin and framed. It sat on his desk as a reminder that Dunkin' Donuts can be more than just for dunkin'.

* * * *

Nils' dad, **"Dutch" Schroeder**, related this story with a lot of paternal pride for his only son. In the years that Nils served on the police force he was never struck down by an enemy bullet.

SECTION SIX

* * * *

The Innocence of Children

PAPER ROUTE ENTREPRENEUR

VINCENT COYLE

It rained so hard that day, poor little Vincent thought he might drown. Four-and-a-half years old and already in a "business" of his own. On his little red three-wheeler, there wasn't a thunderstorm big enough or bad enough to keep him from delivering his papers.

Every afternoon he'd pack up his back seat basket with make-believe editions of the *Philadelphia Inquirer* and the *Evening Bulletin* and start out on his route. His paper route consisted of the perimeter of four blocks surrounding row homes on every side.

His first stop was the corner of Maple Street and Boston Avenue. The corner property had a store front with a huge glass window and an alcove where Vincent would keep his (imaginary) newspapers. Across Boston Avenue was one of the city's largest foundries. One day a foundry worker cupped his hands and yelled across to Vincent,

"Hey kid, why are you getting off and on your bicycle?"

Vincent answered very matter-of-factly, "I'm delivering my newspapers."

"What newspapers?" asked the confounded onlooker.

Vincent never skipped a beat. "*The Evening Bulletin* and *The Inquirer*."

"Ok, then. I need to read the news on my lunch break so bring me a copy of the Bulletin."

"I can't. My mother won't allow me to cross the street." Vincent shot back.

On another delivery Vincent liked to run into Frank Gallagher who owned a casket company. Frank liked Vincent for being such a 'hard-working boy.' Frank was a jovial kind of chap with a broad Irish face and a huge smile. He often reminded Vincent, "Make sure my newspaper is delivered dry everyday, laddie." Then he'd laugh and wink at Vincent as his way of saying, "Keep up the good work, sonny."

On stormy days like today, Vincent always made certain Mr. Gallagher would find a brown bag from the A&P on his front steps with a "newspaper" tucked neatly inside. Vincent was so proud that he satisfied his customers and did his job well.

Maybe all the neighbors didn't know Vincent's last name but they all knew him as "the little newspaper boy." He'd pedal hard because he had a lot of papers to deliver and he didn't want to be late. He wanted every customer to be sure the newspaper would be there waiting when they got home from work.

Even old man Kerrigan's German Shepherd's nasty snarl and gruff barking could not deter Vincent. He was a man on a mission and the papers had to go through. Vincent could see the huge dog pulling on his chain nearly yanking his doghouse out of the ground.

He lowered his head with determination and bravely pedaled even faster until he passed the threatening beast. That dog will have to chew me up and spit me out before I'll stop delivering my newspapers, Vincent thought.

That day he came in the back door dripping wet, his reddish-blonde curly hair in ringlets. He almost looked like a little girl. I couldn't help but smile at him, with his big brown eyes shiny and bright with joy. I'd forgotten that he was outdoors. When I asked why he didn't come inside sooner, he replied, "I was delivering my papers, Mom."

I casually waved him away and said, "Oh, yes. I forgot."

I had to turn my head so he wouldn't catch the look I tried to hide. His forthright honesty caught me off guard and I was forced to smile at this child whose imagination was bigger than himself. After all, he couldn't disappoint his twenty-four customers who lived in the row homes on our street.

No matter how hot it got in summer, how blustery in winter or how soppy in the spring, Vincent showed up every afternoon with a basketful of newspapers because he knew he would work for the newspaper and be a very important person someday.

One day he passed a corner tavern and two men were out front talking. They stood watching as Vincent came down the street, stopping at each house. He'd reach behind his tricycle seat and pull a newspaper from the basket and lay it carefully on the bottom step. One man who had been drinking rather heavily asked the other,

"Wha's that li'l kid doin'?"

The man answered, "Oh, that's Vincent. He delivers newspapers to the neighbors."

The drunk called out, "Hey, kid. Lemme have one of those newspapers."

"Sure," Vincent responded with a smile. Then he added, "Which one do you want, sir? *The Inquirer* or *The Evening Bulletin*?"

To this day I can still hear the other gent laughing.

When his illness kept him from running his paper route, he sold it to a little friend who paid Vincent six lollipops for the "business." More than fifty years later my granddaughter and I were cleaning out some junk in the attic and we came across a box that had once held Vincent's little personal treasures. Inside were the six lollipops from the sale of his imaginary "newspaper business".

* * * *

Ellen Coyle was a feisty Irish lass who raised several children before her recent passing.

THE BATTLE OF THE CENTURY

SANTINO "SONNY" DeNUBILE

YOU KNOW HOW LONG SOME WINTER DAYS can feel when it's dark around 4:30 p.m. and it looks as though it might snow any minute. I remember those days in late November when I dreaded the thought of the long winter months that lay ahead.

Looking up I saw a sky that threatened some heavy snow was about to be dumped on us. I threw another log on the fire and made hot chocolate for Sonny and me and crawled up in an easy chair to watch the flickering flames dance on the logs.

Sonny was a good kid for the most part but there were times when his eight-year-old mischief got a bit out of control. Tonight was one of those times. I wasn't braced for it.

Our dog, Juniper, was just two years old and pretended to be Keeper of the Keys in our castle but more often than not, he was as frisky as Sonny. They were inseparable and I had great faith in Juniper to look after Sonny so they wouldn't get into trouble.

Today was different. Sonny found a small black and white kitten huddling behind our house. He brought it indoors, gave it some milk and a piece of American cheese and asked if we could keep it. I didn't think it was a great idea although the kitten was very pretty and had a sweet disposition. Perhaps we'd find a nice home for him tomorrow. I didn't have the heart to put the kitten out in the cold night air so I said he could stay in the laundry room where it was warm but just for one night. After all, what's one night?

Oh, how I wish I'd never said that. I'm such a soft touch when it comes to furry animals, I couldn't say no to that furball which was purring up against my neck and playing me for all he was worth. I'd never seen such huge green eyes like his and when he looked at me, I began to melt. Ok, so now we're going to keep the kitten, too.

What I hadn't bargained for was Sonny's conjured up scheme to get the two pets acquainted. As I sat in the lounge chair dozing slightly to the sound of the crackling logs, I was thrown out of my chair and nearly hit the ceiling when I heard a cacophony coming from our basement. It sounded like the cat and dog were murdering each other.

Racing to the basement door, I ran down the stairs catching Sonny's raucous laughter as I reached the bottom step. The dog and cat were flying around the room, either trying to catch each other, or get away from each other; I couldn't tell which.

Sonny had tied both their tails together with a small rope and they were about ready to murder each other. The cat's back was arched and he was hissing at Juniper. With his claws extended, his tail whipped back and forth like a fly swatter as he swung the rope up and down. Juniper was barking and screaming and trying to bite the kitten who clawed at Juni's eyes and face with great success leaving gashes that drew his blood.

First, the kitten jumped on a small stool which yanked the rope on Juniper's tail.

Juni bolted and the kitten went flying off the stool. Landing on his feet, the kitten was too quick for Juni. He jumped on Juni's back and dug in. Juni yelped and began running in circles with the kitten hanging on for dear life. The kitten was now flying by the rope in a huge circle sometimes dragging along the floor, sometimes trying to regain his posture and run and sometimes just rolling around. He was truly "at the end of his rope."

In a comedy this would have raised a lot of laughs for how silly they looked but, at that moment, I doubt either one was playing to a full house. Here was a conflict of the species and in some strange way, both were winning. First the kitten, then Juniper.

This chaotic scene went on for several minutes, neither one running out of steam. I was beginning to wonder whether or not they were starting to find the whole thing funny.

It was so comical, I nearly burst out laughing myself. It's a fine line in hysteria that divides the laughing from the crying. I didn't quite know which side I stood on.

I tried to get in the middle but I was getting knotted up between the rope wrapping around my legs as the two crazy ones carried on this wacky performance. Sonny held his sides bursting with laughter.

Grabbing him by the shoulders, I yelled for Sonny to separate the two pets before something terrible happened. We managed to get the cat and dog separated and they slunk off to their respective corners to lick their wounds. Eventually they fell asleep. Glancing around I saw bits of cat fur and dog hair on the floor. The room looked like it hosted the "battle of the century."

Back in the kitchen I sat Sonny down and, in no uncertain terms, I explained what animal cruelty is about. If he ever dared to do anything like that again, I promised him the punishment would be something he wouldn't forget. I don't think he'd ever seen me as angry as I was at that moment. Without remorse, I sent him straight to bed for the night.

During the night I awoke straining my ears for sounds coming from the basement. The next morning I scurried down to the basement to see how the kitten and Juniper were faring. Expecting to see a dead kitten and a seriously wounded dog, I approached with caution. I almost didn't want to look fearing the worst case scenario.

The dog was asleep on his rug and, curled up inside his paws, was the kitten. I could not believe my eyes. I stared in amazement at the pair who were a total contradiction of what had happened the night before. It was like something magical had taken place.

From that day on Juniper and Magic were lifelong buddies. Where one went, the other followed. They ate from the same dish and slept on the same rug. They played in the sunshine and romped in the snowflakes. They rolled and jostled each other in the autumn leaves and played hide-and-seek with Sonny in the spring and summertime.

It was something I could never have imagined, the incredible way in which these two pets became the very best of friends so protective and loving.

Some years later when Sonny went to sleep and never awoke, Juniper and Magic made a secret pact and refused to eat or drink until they died in each other's "arms."

* * * *

Mary DeNubile is residing in upstate New York where she runs a small bed-and-breakfast. She tells this story of great love to anyone who is willing to listen. We hear you, Mary.

THE FISH HOOK

PAUL D'AMICO

IT WAS THE FOURTH OF JULY and the New Jersey seashore resorts were jammed like sardines. On the beach in Wildwood, blankets and sun umbrellas were toe-to-toe. The blistering sun baked everything in its path making it impossible to run from the hot dog stand back to the beach chairs without burning the flesh from the soles of your feet. If I never walk over red-hot coals, I won't be missing anything.

Music blared over the loudspeakers and nearly every hour a lost or found child would be announced from the First Aid Station at Schellenger Avenue and the Boardwalk.

If you hadn't arrived by 10 a.m. you had to park your car five blocks away for lack of parking spaces. Armies of work-weary vacationers compassed their way toward the ocean to find respite from the 9-to-5 world back in their hometowns and cities.

Laden with blankets, chairs, umbrellas, ice chests, sunscreen, radios, rafts, strollers, sand buckets and thermos jugs they came to frolic in the ocean and work on that yearly tan hoping to make their co-workers jealous upon their return to work.

What a fantastic sight to behold! The colorful umbrellas lined the shoreline for as far as your eyes could see. Little children played in the tiny pools left on the shore by the receding tide and sand castles sprung up everywhere. Compromising Daddies allowed themselves to be dutifully buried in the sand as Mom snapped photos of the kids at play.

Oh, what fun it was to lift the tots into the air to jump over the foamy waves that bellied up and moved in toward the beach carrying the proud surfers toward shore on their magnificent surfboards.

The familiar ice cream vendor walked back and forth peddling his popsicles and sandwiches to hungry, sun-burned "lobsters" who were never more willing to pay $1.50 each for that minute of icy pleasure as the creamy stuff slid down their throat like a refreshing waterfall on a steamy summer day.

Everyday our four children were very well instructed to recognize our place on the beach following the boardwalk landmark to keep their direction.

My mother had invited some relatives to spend the day with us and then return to our home for dinner and more of the family gathering. We were a large group of about twenty and we managed our broods with precision and good training. The smaller children knew they were not to wander away from us or go into the ocean without an adult in tow.

However, this day was exceptional. Paul was just four years old and he was playing with other children nearby. When lunchtime rolled around, Nana noticed that Paul was not with that family who had since left the beach. The adults set out in various directions to look for Paul who was nowhere to be seen. I remained at the "camp" with the little ones.

My Dad went up to the hot dog stand to call the First Aid Station in hopes that someone might have taken Paul there and they would announce it over the loud speaker. Many years ago the threat of kidnapping was highly improbable as the crime rate was considerably lower and people were not as suspicious or fearful as we are today. There were no cell phones so we relied upon the public pay phone. (You didn't miss what you didn't have.)

The afternoon began to wear on and I felt panic rising inside me. We questioned several people in the surf but nobody seemed to notice Paul in his little yellow trunks.

My parents took the other smaller children home to bathe them and put them in for a nap. Meanwhile, we kept marching up and down the shoreline hoping to catch a glimpse of Paul. My husband put in a call to the police but they had no way to reach us.

By 5 o'clock most of the people had left the beach and it was easier to scan the area. I tried to appear brave but my trust in the Lord was waning and I began to cry. My heart was squeezed with a sick feeling of despair. I didn't want to think the worst but my little son was missing for hours and now an all-out search of the beach city area was in progress.

It came to me that this was my fault. I allowed myself to be distracted for a short period of time and maybe something terrible was happening to my child at this very moment. It was a wrenching feeling and I felt sick to the pit of my stomach. I retched but nothing came out. My face and head broke out in a sweat and my heart pounded so loud I was certain everyone nearby could hear it.

Were they blaming me as much as I was blaming myself? I wondered. Why was this happening to us? Had I done something terrible, or perhaps it was something that I hadn't done, to deserve this. My thoughts became jumbled and irrational. I tried to appear calm to keep my thoughts aligned but by now I was forcing myself to toss out the horrible pictures that came to my mind as I thought about my darling little boy.

Driving to the Police Station, I cried in my hands. My husband's face was tight with the anguish that gnawed at him as well. He tried to keep cool for my sake and he would not permit himself to think the worst case scenario. I hated myself and my other children would hate me, too, if something tragic had happened to Paul, their little baby brother. He was their favorite after all.

Where was my guardian angel when I needed him most? Maybe he was distracted as well. Was it his day off or was he too busy with other angelic obligations? Ironically, I was tickled at the thought of a guardian angel being overburdened with responsibilities.

Was I crazy or did other people think as I? I tried to sort it all out but I sprung back to reality and I knew I couldn't give this any more head space. I opened myself to what was truth as I knew it and it was not a pretty sight. Over and over I prayed to every saint I could think of and to the Missing Persons Angel Network. I prayed to God Almighty and cursed the devil in the same breath.

But, I wasn't about to give up hope. Somewhere out there my child was crying for his Mommy and I tried hard to psychically tune into that higher energy force hoping to catch a mystical clue which might take us to him. It didn't work. I kept drawing blanks.

At 6 o'clock my husband and I drove to the Police Station to wait for whatever news might come in. The Police Chief knew who we were the instant we walked in by the frantic looks on our faces. We were taut with fear over whatever news may be pending.

He motioned to a nearby door where I heard a familiar sound of my little Paul, whimpering. Dashing into the next room I beheld my beautiful little boy huddled in a blanket, crying. His arm was extended out and he was staring incredulously at a nasty fish hook stuck in his index finger. He was so weary from his ordeal, he couldn't stop crying to acknowledge we were there but he sighed when I gathered him into my arms.

It seems he found a fish hook on the beach and it got stuck under his skin. He tried to remove it and it hurt and bled too much. He was trying to make his way to the First Aid Station on his own and got lost on the beach. A woman found him and brought him to the Police Station. She left her name but no contact number. We had no way to show her our profound gratitude. I was disappointed because I wanted to be forever in her debt.

At the doctor's office, we tried to soothe Paul's pain as the fish hook was removed from his tiny finger. Thirsty and sandy from the beach, I knew he'd appreciate a warm bath and a nap when we got home. I thanked God over and over again that this day had ended so well. There were many lessons to be gleaned from this experience. I knew I would have much to write about in my journal and that this had been a life-altering day.

In the car, I held Paul close to me and stroked his hair and kissed him a hundred times telling him how much we loved him and were so grateful to have him back with us where he belonged. Leaning over, I asked my husband what name the woman gave to the police officer at the station.

His look was far away. He replied in a voice that was almost reverent.

"Angel, just Angel."

* * * *

Carmen D'Amico created the phrase "Angel Parent" and designed its golden emblem. She invites you to write your special story in the next edition of "Angel Parent Memories II".

Carmen lives in Fort Lauderdale, Florida.

ONE BIG HEART, TWO LITTLE SOLES

H. COREY WYNGRAM

MY WIFE, FAY, always had a difficult time when it came to buying shoes for our son, Corey. He hated Oxford-type shoes and Fay always wanted him to wear Buster Browns.

At four years of age, Corey thought of himself as a pro baseball player so he wanted absolutely nothing to do with shoes that resembled anything sensible. His idea of shoes meant something with cleats. He even would have welcomed a pair of combat boots over laces or those hideous Buster Browns. Fay would not hear of it.

School opened and Corey was walked to pre-school with his little schoolbag slung over one shoulder, a baseball cap and, you guessed it, those awful Buster Brown shoes.

Fay kept trying to take Corey's mind off his shoes by enumerating all the great things he'd find to love about pre-school. Corey's scowl told her she was not making any progress.

Fay kissed Corey on his cheek, turned the beak on his baseball cap to the front and left him at the school steps. Waving him off, Fay felt a little twinge of separation coaxing a tear from her eye. She deliberately didn't look back so she wouldn't have to see that face with the frown from here to there. She made her way homeward in the hope other boys would be wearing Buster Browns also, so Corey wouldn't stand out like a sore thumb.

The day went well; no phone calls from the principal's office. Fay sighed with relief. She busied herself making Corey's favorite chocolate and vanilla pudding parfaits so they could sit and he could tell her all about his first day at school.

She called me twice to chat but I could tell she was more concerned about Corey's first school day than she was about the fact she wanted me to pick up some dinner rolls after work. I didn't question her feelings but I knew how much Corey disliked his shoes and I didn't want to elaborate on it.

"Fay, I'm home!" I sang out as I came in from the driveway. When Fay entered the kitchen, I could tell it wasn't all she had hoped for. She looked annoyed and puzzled.

"Is something wrong, hon? Where's Corey?" I tried to appear nonchalant.

"Oh, Corey's fine. The day went okay, I suppose, but somehow he's lost his shoes."

Fay was wiping her hands on her apron and she seemed fidgety.

"He said he 'lost his shoes' and I couldn't get anything else out of him. You try."

I found Corey in front of the TV in the living-room, content and shoeless. No socks, either. He looked okay, not like he'd been roughed up or anything. I sat next to him.

"Hey, Corey. Now both of Mommy's guys are keeping busy at work and at school. It must have felt kind of lonesome around here today for her. How was school?"

Corey looked me square in the eyes and said very matter-of-factly, "Okay, Daddy. School was okay but I don't have my shoes anymore." He didn't seem a bit upset.

"What happened to them? They didn't just disappear. Where are they, Corey?"

"They got lost, Daddy. But, it's okay, 'cause I didn't like them anyhow. I only had them because Mommy made me wear them, but I sure didn't like them one bit."

"Corey, I know you don't care for the shoes but you have to tell me where they are. You know, there are little boys just like you somewhere in Asia who don't know what a pair of shoes feels like because their family is too poor to buy them nice shoes. I think you should tell me what happened to the shoes even if you don't like them."

"C'mon, Daddy, I'll show you." He was being very diplomatic with me.

He put on his older shoes and we went outside. Taking my hand, he led me to the courtyard surrounding the hospital down the block from our house. I wondered what he was doing that far from the house and I questioned him.

"Corey, what were you doing this far from home when you were supposed to be on the bus after school? Mommy would have been very upset if she knew you'd walked this far by yourself. I don't want you to do that ever again without permission."

"Ok, Daddy. Over there." He pointed to a flower bed behind the high metal fence.

"I threw them over there. Do we have to tell Mommy? She's going to be really mad at me."

"I think Mommy needs to know what happens to the things we buy for you and we don't want you throwing your shoes away, or anything else, for that matter. This isn't going to happen again, Corey, do you understand? Mommy and I won't put up with this sort of thing, not now, not anytime, is that clear?"

"Ok, Daddy. I won't throw anything away without telling you and Mommy."

We walked almost the entire perimeter of the fenced yard. Once inside the gate, we walked all the way back to where Corey had tossed his shoes. In the flower bed the shoes lay there waiting for us. I picked them up and we went home to explain it all to Fay.

The next few days went alright but we could tell Corey still had no love for those Buster Brown shoes. The minute he got in the door, he changed into his older shoes.

On Friday I walked into the kitchen and Fay was standing with her hands on her hips, fuming. "He did it again! He came home without his shoes. He said he wouldn't tell me where they went until you got home. Harry, I don't like this one bit and I don't think it's one bit humorous! I made him go to his room. I think we better get this ironed out right now. I don't want to tolerate any more pranks like this. I'm...."

I could see her eyes getting misty and she was very upset. I interrupted.

"Fay, I'll take care of this. Calm down. I know we'll find out what he did with his shoes. And for Pete's sake, don't buy him anymore of those darn Buster Browns. If you want the truth, I never liked them myself."

I called up the stairs to Corey who came running out his room at once.

"Hi, Daddy! Boy, am I glad you're home. Mommy's mad at me again and she made me stay in my room."

He came bouncing down the steps and threw himself into my arms.

"Hey, big guy! What's going on with the shoes? Mommy said you came home again without your new shoes. Didn't I tell you I didn't want this to happen again?"

"But, Daddy. You said the kids in Asia didn't have any shoes and today, there was a new kid in my class and his shoes were all beat up and had holes in them and the laces were all in knots. So, I gave him my new shoes. Isn't that great, Dad? Now at least one kid from Asia has new shoes!"

This time it was my eyes that got all misty and there was a lump in my throat.

My heart swelled with pride. I learned a lesson in charity from my little son that day. I thought, I hope he never loses the goodness of helping others.

"Get your jacket, Corey. We're going out to buy you a different pair of shoes."

* * * *

Harry Wyngram looks back on the little photo Fay took of Corey on his first day of nursery school. Corey was wearing his Buster Brown shoes.

THE WRINGER'S A HUM DINGER

FLORA D'IPPOLITO

BACK IN 1939 THE BLUE COLLAR household had a lot to be desired. We were thankful for what we had but, an extra ten dollars would have helped a lot. Getting back on your feet after the Depression wasn't easy. With three little girls not yet in kindergarten, I really had my hands full. Luckily my husband had a job while so many other able-bodied men stood in breadlines for hours in hopes of not going home empty-handed to their needy families.

It was a time when people everywhere in America were scarred with the remnants of the Depression. No matter how hard you worked to acquire something extra, it just wasn't there to be had even if you were fortunate to earn the money. Necessities had to come first!

I recall one week when my husband brought home a meager four dollars, a pitiful sum. I was grateful nonetheless. We gave two dollars to the family across the street because they also had a little child and there wasn't any food in their cupboard. It was no sacrifice.

My thoughts were running away with me so I turned my attention back to the pile of dirty laundry. I brushed away a tear and pushed back my hair into the bun which was coming loose. Too often I had those mixed emotions when a tear meant I was unhappy for so many of the people we knew. At the same time, I was grateful for our lot.

As I recall January was exceptionally rainy that year and it was difficult trying to keep the house dry as well as warm. I lit the oven as often as possible to bake bread or meatloaf so the girls could stay in the kitchen with coloring books or play with paper dolls.

That Monday morning was like all other Mondays. I guessed every woman in South Philadelphia was washing her clothes in the basement, if she were lucky enough to have a wringer-type washing machine. Some women still had to use a washboard. Looking back I ask myself what was so good about "the good old days?"

Flora was three at the time and she seemed to cling to me more than the other two. Being the middle child had little bearing on her. She was the spunky one, sang a little louder and claimed more territory than she needed. Sometimes I wondered if her wavy hair wasn't the result of her wiry personality.

Running towels through the winger was heavier work than pillowcases so, as the galvanized tub filled up, I tried to keep up by hanging the towels on clotheslines with wooden clothes pins. I didn't want her help, yet Flora kept insisting she help me with the laundry. She persisted in offering the logic that she was big enough to do "grown up things" so I should enlist her assistance and together, we could get the job done faster.

She'd be at my heels constantly handing me things to prove her capability. What I wanted more was for her to join her sisters who were playing with their dollies.

The coal furnace was running full blast so it was kind of cozy in the basement in spite of the bitter, wet cold of the still-dark morning. A shovel of coal from the coal bin was enough to stoke the furnace just a tad and I checked to see if there was enough hot water to finish the wash.

Usually the girls and I would sing or hum to make the work go easier. I was nearing the end of the second load of clothes when a high-pitched scream filled the basement. My blood curdled.

As I spun around, I could see Flora's little arm going through the wringer. She had tried to put one of her Daddy's handkerchiefs through the wringer and it got caught around the roller.

When she tried to catch the corner to pull it away, her tiny fingers rolled into the wringer and it wouldn't release her. Her arm proceeded to roll through and she was screaming at the top of her lungs. Instantly I was at her side, trying frantically to stop the rollers but they were stuck fast. I tried to pull her arm out and she screamed even more, crying and trying to pry herself loose with her other hand. I was so afraid her other arm would get caught, too. I'm certain I was as terrified as she that very moment. Her sisters were screaming. It sounded like a House of Horrors with everyone yelling.

I tried to reach the "stop" switch but I just couldn't feel it around the outer bottom of the tub. Flora's body was wedged between the washer and the wall so I couldn't get back there to pull the plug. I couldn't remove the little stool she was standing on or she'd remain hanging in place by her injured arm.

Oh, dear God, her arm will be crushed! Terrible thoughts raced through my mind and I felt myself panicking. I was always so careful, I blamed myself. How could this happen? There's noone around to help. We had no 'phone back then. I knew my neighbor wasn't at home. She was visiting her mother in New Jersey. I never felt so helpless in my life!

"MOMMY, MOMMY, HELP ME! Please don't make me die!" she cried. The shock of that terrible possibility gripped my heart and I heard myself let out an anguished sob.

"Oh, my baby, my baby!" Tears were streaming down our faces and my stomach was in one enormous knot. It was like my worst nightmare coming true.

The girls were screaming, "Mommy, help her, help her!" They were jumping in front of me trying to get to their sister and they only hindered my attempts to free Flora's arm. I couldn't get them away from me and Flora, so I swung my arm out in desperation and they both fell to the floor, crying with surprise and shock over what was happening. For a split second I hated myself but I knew I had to free Flora's arm before more damage occurred. The scene was utter bedlam. Everyone was hysterical. I felt nothing but self-loathing for what I had just done and for not being in control of a situation over which I had no control, no matter what. Then it dawned on me. This was no time for self-evaluations and I called on my guardian angel to help me and my children.

Then with all my might, I jerked the washing machine so hard that the plug fell out of the wall. It stopped the machine from running so the rollers came to a dead halt. It was nearly impossible to pry the rollers apart with my child's arm stuck in between and the rollers had taken her arm in up above her elbow.

I saw her fingers turning blue. She looked as if she was about to faint. A layer of her skin was peeled away from the pressure of the rollers and her arm was bright pink and angry-looking. Her fingertips and nails had turned bluish-purple.

I looked up and begged, "Somebody, please help me!" As if I'd discovered a vault of stored energy, I took my shoe and whacked at the rollers with such force, they simply came apart. Swiftly and gently I removed Flora's injured arm.

I ordered the other girls to go upstairs and sit in the kitchen and told them not to move until I got home. I'd find someone to come in while I was gone. They were holding onto each other, still crying, fearful and confused at the drama that had just taken place.

I flung my winter coat around Flora's body, yelled across the street for another neighbor to come in and mind the girls. I ran down the street with my baby who had fainted now. I couldn't tell if she were alive or...Oh, God, don't let me even think it.

It was full daylight now and the gusting wind and rain soaked my body instantly. I crunched through old piles of slush still frozen on the sidewalks and my feet felt like they were instantly iced from the needles that pricked my toes and ankles.

Sobbing as I ran, I noticed people waiting for streetcars staring at me, unable to help as they had to get to their places in the soup kitchens or nearby welfare stations. I didn't know if I was sorrier for their plight or mine at that moment.

The needling rain pelted my face and blurred my vision.

Run, just keep running, I thought. Just then I caught a patch of ice and fell on my knees. A fierce, stinging sensation burned my kneecaps as I struggled to regain my stature. I hit the ground with such force I thought I broke something yet I hugged that little girl so tightly, I almost forgot the pain in my legs.

It wasn't until later that I saw the frozen blood on my leg that had traced its path down toward my ankle. It felt all hot and cold at the same time but it didn't hurt any more than my lungs which were freezing from the icy wind, and my body which was heated up from running so hard.

Around the next corner was St. Agnes Hospital, a blessing in disguise. It seemed to be miles away today and I felt like I ran forever until I saw that familiar sign. I raced past everything and everyone and fled toward the Emergency Room.

At the reception desk a pristine nurse in a starched white uniform with white stockings and a sparkling nurse's cap stared at me in disbelief.

As I flew past her, she jumped up, waving her arms frantically.

"Oh, madam, no, no, you can't go in there! Wait, wait...I need to get some information first...!"

I wasn't about to ask whether or not there was an emergency operation going on in the OR. I burst through those doors and literally dumped Flora's limp body on the table.

At once nurses and attendants swarmed around my child and I got pushed into the background as the sounds of instruments clanged and a lot of hustle and bustle took over.

I fell into the nearest chair, sobbing relentlessly as I tried to explain what had transpired. I guess it sounded pretty awful, ".....rollers...baby's arm...whacked the machine...the kids were in my way..." Probably none of it made any sense to them.

All I wanted to know was whether my baby would live or die. Like any mother, I was entrenched in Flora's crisis, yet too scared to see what was going on.

They assured me she would be alright as soon as the doctors could set her broken arm and they had finished administering medications and arm dressings.

I imagined she wouldn't have just a broken arm, perhaps a case of pneumonia had set in. I thought, I'm acting like a crazy woman. Get hold of yourself!

I cut myself some slack for permissible hysteria. I'm allowed, I thought. After all, isn't blood thicker than water? What did they know about how I felt? I forgave myself and them a little and moved into the background so the pros could do what they did best.

All at once my teeth began to chatter and I felt the cold and dampness go through me. Someone wrapped a woolen blanket around me and stuck a thermometer in my mouth.

I managed to swallow the water a nurse handed me. I wondered if I'd ever be able to forgive myself for allowing this to happen. It was then she noticed my bloody leg and cleaned it up not long before another doctor put some sutures on the kneecap.

I felt a little heady to I took a few breaths and told myself not to pass out. I winced as the catgut burned through my skin but I thought I'd better shut up before I'm labeled a coward in the face of what had just happened to poor little Flora.

Looking around I saw other people also waiting for treatment. No one made a move to come near me; they all had their own problems. A man with blood oozing from his head sat across from me rocking back and forth moaning. Someone was throwing up in the bathroom and the room reeked of ether. The green walls didn't do much for the atmosphere either. The sirens of ambulances arriving in a steady stream were a sign I was living a sheltered life in our little house and I had a lot more to be thankful for.

Now as I sat in the waiting room, I ran a dozen Hail Mary's through my head and promised myself I'd send out the laundry from now on even if I had to sew clothes for my neighbors to pay the bill. I wondered if my little girl would ever have the use of her arm again. I had to leave it all up to God and the doctors and nurses.

It was hard to believe I'd only been awake for a few hours. It seemed like years. So many things occurred that brought me to this place. Not my usual routine. The whole thing ran amok in my mind and I felt exhausted. I needed to lie down.

Nearly ninety minutes went dragging by before I could see my daughter. I tried to be brave. After all, how could I let her see me so disheveled and red-eyed? I needed to be strong for her. Wasn't she going to need me a lot more now? Oh, how I hated that awful smell. It was enough to make you nauseous even if you weren't.

Finally, a short, chubby blonde nurse in an OR gown came shuffling into the room, her feet covered in surgery socks over her white shoes. She smiled. In a thick, southern accent she told me that "mah chile" was gonna be singin' "Skip to mah Lu" 'fore long.' "

I was ushered to her bedside in the little cubicle. When I pushed aside the curtain, I saw my darling sitting up smiling. She had one arm in a plaster cast, supported with a cheesecloth type of sling. The other held a cherry lollipop to her lips. Amazing, I thought, how a simple antidote like a lollipop could heal a broken arm faster and reduce the pain more quickly than my poor, aching heart. Silently I counted another gray hair on my head. I must have looked like an absolute wreck with my rumpled dress and damp hair.

"Hi, Mommy!" she cried out as I stepped up to her bedside. She held out her good arm to embrace me. You would think she had seen an angel, but it was only me.

"The doctor said I can go home soon, if I promise never to put my arm through the rollers again. He said I should wait to wash clothes 'til I'm a big girl like you." I exhaled.

When the doctor drew me aside to give me a prescription for pain and some fatherly advice, he added, "Your daughter is quite a little lady. She said if it weren't for you pulling the cord from the washing machine, she would have been pulled through the rollers and come out 'flattened like a pancake.' She said that as much as she loves pancakes, she didn't want to be rolled out like one." We both managed a laugh.

I was more surprised the next day. Flora suggested that maybe we should try flattening the clothes through the rollers when they were dry and then I wouldn't have to iron them.

Nice try, I thought but I wasn't buying any more of her "adult wisdom." I'd had enough infantile "logic" for one day.

* * * *

(Note: **Jennie D'Ippolito**, 95, may be the oldest woman in America to be published for the very first time. This story was recounted to the author by Mrs. D'Ippolito with great drama and recollection. She is my mother and Flora was my older sister.)

—**Carmen D'Amico**

SECTION SEVEN

* * * *

Teaching and Learning

A PLAN FOR TONY

ANTHONY DANILKO

WELL, I'LL BE DARNED, I thought. Wouldn't you know it...I had just sold the baby crib because my doctor assured me I couldn't become pregnant again. Scott 'n' Matt were 4-1/2 and 6 and I was preparing to go back to work. When that usual backache returned along with an ample dose of morning sickness, I knew it was time to think diapers again.

They'd ask the usual questions like, "How much longer 'til the baby comes, Mommy? How will he get out of your tummy so we can play with him?" On February 28th I was certain this child would have an old-fashioned birth date, but God had a plan for Tony. He arrived right smack in the middle of Leap Year Day!

Scott 'n' Matt were awed with the whole baby scene and they played with Tony and loved him like he was a little puppy, only more. Tony was always our special little guy.

In 1981 we moved to sunny Florida but Tony didn't adjust well. He missed his grandparents very much and he wanted to return to his Catholic school so we permitted him to go up north to finish fifth grade. He loved it but I was suffering without him.

God had a plan for Tony on the morning he made his First Communion. I flew north to surprise him and he was so happy, he decided to come back to stay with me in Florida. I never wanted him to be away from me again.

As time passed Tony discovered surfboarding was far more exhilarating than skateboarding. He'd spend hours watching the weather channel to know when the surf was up. In a flash he and his surfer buddies would hit the beach. Even on the day Hurricane Andrew was threatening the east Florida coastline in 1992, Tony and his friends were on their boards. He made up his mind he would go anywhere in the world to be there when the surf would be "up."

Tony went to Barbados, Costa Rica, rode the big ones in California, the smaller ones in Florida and fulfilled his greatest dream when he surfed Puerto Rico. Tony knew as long as he lived near an ocean, it would beckon to him.

The next call Tony felt was to be closer to his brother, Matt, so he went to Norfolk, Virginia where Matt was living. Matt had gone to Palm Beach Atlantic Christian College and he learned about God and His Word with the Bible very thoroughly. It was then Tony felt Matt could help him guide his career. Matt shared with Tony all that he had learned in his Bible studies and Tony listened intently, soaking up this knowledge like a sponge.

During one of their private discussions, Tony revealed a deep secret. He told Matt he had a strong feeling that he would not live to see his old age. The news neither surprised nor frightened Matt as he had come to believe in his faith. Matt never doubted God's plans for us. When Tony left Matt, he locked all the new wisdom in his heart.

Tony saved money for a "one way ticket" and went to Puerto Rico with a brand new surf board tucked under his arm and a job section of the newspaper under the other.

After surfing and sunsets Tony would gather with close friends around campfires on the beach. In the soft glint of firelight, Tony looked like a golden-haired Gentle Giant who spoke from the depths of his heart to his friends who loved him. His blue eyes sparkled as he spoke about his love for the Lord. Under starry skies Tony would minister to them with spiritual stories to enthrall them and lead their hearts and minds toward our Lord, Jesus Christ.

In 1995 Tony returned home from the surf fest in Puerto Rico. No longer was he the young boy I remembered. Now he was a man with a steady gaze and determination to continue his life in a more serious manner.

Eventually Tony joined the Navy and God had a plan for Tony. He was going to be stationed in Hawaii. Who could ask for more?

Tony said, "Now I have everything I've ever dreamed of."

As before, God had a plan for Tony. I am sure He said, "My son, you are so right with the world, but I have a special place for you here with Me. Now it is time to put away your surfboard for soon you shall have wings." That was God's plan for Tony.

FOR MY BROTHER, TONY

"Won't you take me for a fly?"
You smile that way with new found pride.
"What they said was right on time —
These wings are real, They're really mine."
"And that's not all, There's plenty more.
You've no idea of what's in store.
Songs of praise and feasts for kings,
Wedding bells and shiny things.
So please don't ever cry for me —
I'm far from lost. I'm home, I'm free."

—Matthew C. Danilko, May 1995

* * * *

Diane Silverman spent several years building her reputation with "The Mystic Hill Cattery," her breeding home of grand champion felines with fancy bloodlines. Diane loves to read and relax on Florida's cruise ships when she's not dining out with her husband, Lou. They live in Boca Raton, Florida.

JULIA CHILD SHE AIN'T

LILY BENSON-WRIGHT

WHENEVER IT CAME time to bake chocolate chip cookies or an apple pie, Lily would drop whatever she was doing and run into the kitchen to help with the baking. From the time she could walk she loved playing with wooden spoons and spatulas while Mom mixed and blended and iced a cake. What kid didn't like licking the icing off the spoon?

Lily showed early signs of a future chef and Mother Beverly had all kinds of dreams that perhaps one day Lily would grow up to have a restaurant or bakery of her own.

By the time Lily was thirteen, Beverly thought it might be time for her to try some things on her own so Lily could learn to comprehend recipes, measurements and culinary terminology.

On the day when Beverly was going to spend some time at the dentist, she left a note for Lily to follow her instructions and prepare a simple dish for the evening meal.

Lily took things from the pantry and refrigerator and assembled them neatly on the counter. She took out serving dishes, utensils, pots and pans and opened the cookbook. This is going to be a lot of fun, Lily thought. I'll make Mom so proud of me.

After cleaning a few vegetables with just the slightest nick to her finger, Lily put 1/4 cup of cooking oil into a large pan to saute some sliced onions. She was going to serve up the most surprising meal. She put on a pot of water to boil for some pasta, put a lid on it and she was just about to pick up the recipe when the phone rang.

Lily told her girlfriend she was cooking the evening meal and didn't have much time to talk. Her girlfriend asked her to look up something in a reference book they were using for that night's homework, so Lily walked into the den and picked up her briefcase.

She began to give her girlfriend the information she wanted when her friend asked her about the Saturday night dance at school. They went on to talk about the boys who would probably be there and what they'd planned to wear to the dance. Then the conversation turned to other things and they began to laugh and went on talking.

Suddenly there was a huge puffing sound like a paper bag being popped. As Lily looked toward the kitchen, she saw a burst of flames from the burning fry pan leap up the wall of cabinets. Lily let out a scream and dropped the phone.

The flames spread rapidly and within seconds the curtains were burning. She ran back into the den but she couldn't find the phone which had fallen into a magazine rack minutes earlier.

She began screaming at the sight of the flames but somehow she was mesmerized by the sight. The flames moved rapidly above the kitchen cabinets, burning the collection of cookbooks on the top shelf. Quickly the flames ate everything in sight. Lily was stunned and frightened. She ran outdoors and ran to a neighbor's house. There was no one home.

Then she ran across the street screaming for help but those neighbors were not at home, either. A passing car stopped and dialed 911 while Lily was sobbing hysterically on the sidewalk.

Now the flames could be seen from the street and they were moving into the dining-room. Just then the sound of fire engines were near and soon they came into view.

Within minutes the house was transformed into a small inferno. Lily's mother drove up. She ran to Lily, crying in each other's arms yet happy she was safe and sound.

Lily tried to tell her mother what happened but she was shaking uncontrollably. Within ten minutes the entire neighborhood was gathering around to offer help. Eventually, the fire was under control. Lily's family began eating out often after that.

A few months later the Benson household had a newly renovated kitchen and a serious debt for about twenty-five thousand dollars.

Beverly swore Lily would not attempt to do anything other than make toast or pop tarts and hot tea unless someone was in the kitchen with her. Lily was grounded for her lack of responsibility and spent a lot of time hand-washing dishes until they had a new dishwasher installed.

Beverly was amazed at how wrong she guessed Lily's talents might be. It was certain: Julia Child, she ain't!

* * * *

Beverly and her husband, **Mark**, live in a small town in Oregon with another daughter, Phyllis and their dog, Pinky.

DON'T GIVE ME A RASH

DAVID SCHOFIELD

SOME KIDS HAVE TO BE THE center of attention. If it meant breaking a leg while jumping off a roof to get attention, they might do it or die trying.

David Schofield was no exception to this rule. Once I remember when he painted his entire head of hair with red ink just to show off. He thought he'd get a laugh and he did. He also got a suspension from school and a month of detentions.

Another time he wanted to make some money on a dare to drop his pants in front of a senior female who took all the honors in school. She also was shy and easily embarrassed. He must have picked the right day. When he called her name, she turned around, he dropped his knickers and, lo and behold! It was the substitute teacher. Egad! That set him back about 5000 points in the popularity department.

It appeared that David had learned a few lessons as he managed to stay pretty low key that semester. That is, until the day of the Autumn Hike, an all-day expedition in the woods with all the senior classes.

Under the direction of their class sponsor, the students spent the entire day honing their forest skills in marking trails, searching for food under dire conditions and making rescue stretchers for an "injured" student. It was like an adult Boy Scout project.

Among the students there was a young girl named Rosemary who had just come to the school that same year. She was a very pretty girl who made very good grades. She was an only child and her parents were quite proud of her even though she was a bit spoiled.

Unlike a lot of seniors, David wanted to make an impression on Rosemary so he conjured up a little scheme. He planned to hide in a certain area of bushes and ground cover so when the girls were nearby, David would come crawling out as if he were unable to walk. Then they'd have to make a stretcher for him and he would get some personal attention from Rosemary. He knew the plan could work like a charm.

As the groups went in various directions, David went on ahead to hide as he planned. He laid on the ground and waited. A period of time went by and David began to get impatient. The mosquitoes must have been especially hungry that day for he began to itch behind his neck and around his face and arms. Still he waited.

When the girls finally drew closer to the area where he'd been hiding, David began to moan and he slowly crawled out from under the brush. When the girls saw him, a few of them looked strangely surprised.

David complained in a very dramatic-sounding voice that he'd hurt his ankle and he was unable to walk any further. He supposed they'd have to create a stretcher and carry him back to the campsite.

Looking at him, a few of the girls didn't want to touch him. He didn't look very well at all. One of them decided to run back to the counselor to ask for help. David was looking very red, swollen and weird.

Once back at the campsite, the counselor took a look at him and he knew David needed to be rushed to a hospital. He felt very hot and his lips were thick and reddened. He had a dry throat and his arms had nasty red patches on them.

Imagine his embarrassment when he was diagnosed with a case of poison ivy.

* * * *

David's mother, **Clare MacKenzie**, remembers how Rosemary never gave David a second glance. That might have been just the remedy he needed to attain a more subdued personality. She lives with her terrier, Dolly, outside of Des Moines, Iowa. Mrs. MacKenzie is employed by a film developing company.

YOU WIN SOME, YOU LOSE SOME

SALLY DVORAK

NO MATTER WHAT YOU DO in life to earn your living, you have to love your work.

My mother used to say that to me when I was a young woman and that's what I told my daughter when she was a teenager.

Sally wanted to go to school to study interior design. From the time she was very young, I always remember her wanting to rearrange the furniture and cabinets. It did not matter how often she changed things, she always thought it would look better placed in a different pattern. I learned early on not to walk about the house in the dark. I'd fall over some footstool or knock something over that wasn't there yesterday.

Sally worked in a local upholstery warehouse to help pay for her tuition. On weekends she would hire herself out as a junior decorator for a very small fee just to practice whatever she'd learned that month in school. I can't say I always loved her mod tastes for certain wallpapers and accessories but then, I was somewhat of a traditionalist and not very nervy when it came to change.

She came home one day and announced that it was time for me to change my old ideas about the house furnishings and go with something new and entirely different. She described how we could refinish the furniture and use some new fabrics to recover the sofa and chairs.

She had access to some remnants for draperies and we would get a substantial discount if we bought a few new area rugs from the warehouse where she worked. She even offered to repaint the walls if I'd agree to get rid of that "nasty-looking wallpaper" as she described it. Reluctantly, I agreed. I didn't know how long she'd work at the warehouse and the furnishings certainly were a bargain considering her discount.

Sally took me to the warehouse one Saturday and we spent nearly a whole day picking out different looks, color schemes and patterns. Come to think of it, I was having a fun time. I had to agree with her; enough years had gone by and our tired living-room certainly deserved a facelift.

Then we were off to the paint store to select some blended colors that sounded more like summer fruits than pastel paints. Colors like Mocha Magic, Pears 'n' Praline and Fuzzy Navel for peach intrigued me and got my mouth salivating.

Armed with an arsenal of decorating paraphernalia, we looked like a small team of professional decorators as we entered our humble little home. After seeing so many new color and fabric treatments, I looked around and realized Sally was right. I'd been long overdue for a change of decor. It was almost a relief now that someone had pushed me to make up my mind and go bold.

Tossing fabrics on sofa, chairs and windows, Sally prattled on about how much happier I'd be once the job was done. I sheepishly agreed she was right again.

Rolling up the old area rugs, I felt a slight twinge of pain at the thought of parting with them. They were like old friends to me but I shrugged my shoulders and gave up. I guessed by now it was easier to be led around than stumble around in a quandary.

Sally and I agreed to take off a whole week and just redo everything we'd planned so we could get the job done faster. I literally rolled up my sleeves and took a deep breath. This was bound to be an experience I'd not soon forget.

I was awakened the next morning by some strange sounds coming from the living-room. It sounded as if something were being sheared, a ripping kind of noise.

Stepping out of the bedroom, I was jolted into reality. Sally was tearing the paper off the walls as fast as she could. I guess she didn't want to give me time to change my mind. The sight of the bare walls stunned me a little at first and seeing all the furniture piled up in the center of the room shocked me. I'd been used to seeing everything in place exactly as I'd left it for so many years.

"Oh, hi, Mom. I wanted to get an early start. Why don't you put on a pot of coffee and a work shirt and we can get this junk out of here by noontime," Sally said.

Unable to respond, I went about obeying my orders like a robot. I was almost too stunned to say anything because I wasn't sure if I'd made a right decision.

The area rugs were rolled up, waiting on the sidelines. Waiting for what? I thought. Waiting for the trash collector, seemed the logical answer.

Walking into the living-room, I handed Sally a coffee mug and flopped into a chair.

"This place is going to look so good, you'll think you're in the wrong house when you come from work," Sally went on.

"I'm sending the furniture to the warehouse to be redone so it won't be in our way while we're painting and doing the other stuff. They'll keep it for a few weeks and by the time it's ready, the walls will be painted and the draperies will be hung."

"I already promised some of these old pieces to a few people I know and you can do with a lot less clutter. It'll expand the room and the open window treatments will let in a lot more light."

I was having visions of my drained bank account and a mounting credit card debt.

"Oh, Sally, don't you think you're rushing this a bit? I don't know if I can afford to get rid of some furniture. What'll I do to replace it? And what about those rugs?"

"Ok, Mom, do we just want to go back to what you had? Maybe we should just put some new area rugs over the old area rugs, just in case you have a change of heart?"

I realized how silly I sounded. I sighed and nodded in agreement.

On Monday morning the furniture was picked up, area rugs tossed, draperies, cushions and other things were donated to Goodwill. Huge trash bins stood at the curb brimming with outdated wallpaper shreds, old kitchen hardware, pots and pans.

Looking around I felt a sense of freedom and feeling relief that I wouldn't have to spend a lot of time dusting and scouring those old things. This was turning out to be fun after all. I caught myself looking forward to the surprising new look of the furniture.

Sally had sent out the dining-room and living-room pieces together so their finishes would have a subtle blend to complement each other. I felt my heart quicken.

Later that afternoon, she walked in with an enormous box in her arms. It was a little like a surprise birthday party and I was getting all the presents.

"Mom, wait 'til you see what I picked up for a song." Sally was beaming.

Out came a beautiful hanging lamp for over the dining-room table. I smiled.

"I just couldn't resist it so I thought we could finally dump this old thing," she said, pointing to the outdated poor excuse for a chandelier. I had to agree its time had come.

We worked tirelessly that entire week. Never having held a paintbrush before, I was wearing nearly as much paint as I managed to roll on the walls. I soon got the hang of it and by the time we were finished, I felt like I could tackle the bathroom walls on my own.

We picked up some great bargain remnant carpets and the room began to take on a whole new look. It was enchanting to see such transformation. It was like watching a TV show about my own house and it made me giggle that I was giving my home the facelift of the century. I began poring over decorating magazines like never before.

Over the weeks that followed, I began to get restless about the delays in getting back the furniture. Sally made numerous calls and she was told they were so backed up with other work, there'd be some delays but that they would be delivering my beautiful, newly refinished furniture the following week.

Sally caught cold that same week. She couldn't go to school or to work. She stayed at home and put in a little effort to put things back in place; but, her cold took the starch out of her and she spent a few days in bed.

Nearly four weeks had passed by now and the furniture was yet to be seen. I made a few calls and the machine took messages but no one returned my calls. I began to get angry and decided we should go down to the warehouse to see if there was a problem.

Pulling up to the warehouse, Sally and I were stunned beyond belief. The building was closed, doors locked, no cars in sight, deserted, shut down tight. I was speechless.

It was Monday and no one at the adjoining warehouses seemed to know anything about the whereabouts of the owners, the furnishings or the stark appearance of this once-busy enterprise. I felt bushwhacked.

After hundreds of phone calls, letters, attorney's notices and fruitless attempts, we were not surprised to see the local TV news reports that the furniture dealer/refinishers had been arrested on charges of theft and resale of stolen goods.

Sally and I were shocked. The long drawn-out procedure to recoup our losses had drained our energies and bank accounts. We never recovered our furniture.

On the brighter side, Sally and I learned how to shop the flea markets, local consignment shops, Goodwill bargain stores and furniture finds. We became experts in furniture refinishing and chair re-upholstering. I must say we have a far more beautiful place than we ever expected and all the while, our guardian angels came to our rescue.

In the grand scheme of things, I chalked it up to the fact that somewhere, someone got my old furniture. I hope they needed it more than I.

Years later Sally and I laughed a lot about that experience and to this day, I try to see the fortune in our misfortune. They say that things happen for the best. I agree.

Sally went on to finish her course in interior design but she never attempted to redo a house for me or even so much as recover a throw pillow.

This was more fun anyhow. And, I learned a lot from this life experience.

* * * *

Sally's mother, **Anita**, and her husband of recent years, live in Toledo, Ohio. She has a hobby re-finishing wicker and rattan furniture but she leaves the expensive pieces to the professionals. She brags that she wields a "pretty mean paintbrush."

TRAIN FOR SALE

FLOYD CORBELLAN

FROM THE TIME he was two, Floyd Maurice Corbellan wanted a set of toy trains.

His Daddy had taken him to a "Trains 'n' Planes" Trade Show and from that first day, Floyd knew in his little heart he wanted to fill his life with trains. Daddy couldn't buy him a real train so Floyd had to settle for the next best thing: an authentic train whistle.

Little did Floyd's Daddy or Mommy know, even in their wildest dreams, that theirs would become a lifetime of the trains from Hell.

From the moment he got home from the trade show, he bombarded his Mommy with talk about "those gi-antic trains." Floyd marched all around the house blowing that train whistle and shouting "All aboard!" like a train conductor. He had no idea what that was all about. He just knew he liked everything about the trains and he was going to grow into them for all he was worth.

The whistle-blowing wasn't all that terrible for the first ten minutes. In fact, his Mommy thought it sounded kind of cute. Imagine Floyd dressed up in a little striped pair of train engineers pants and a matching hat like the engineers wore. He would look so adorable with his little curly hair poking out from under the hat. She entertained the mental pictures she had of him strutting around swinging a little lantern in his hand.

"Whooo! Whooo! Here comes the train! Make way for the train!" he'd yell.

Up and down he marched blowing his train whistle and smiling from ear to ear.

By this time Mommy was beginning to think that Daddy had created a monster. She gave herself a count to ten, took a deep breath, and in her sweetest voice laced with arsenic, she said to Floyd, "Ok, honey, it's been a lot of fun but now Mommy has a headache and it's time to put away the train whistle. You can play with it again tomorrow."

Well, if you never saw a miniature train engineer throw a calculated fit, you were about to see one now. Floyd began to cry and he put up quite a fight before the defeat of calling it a night and being tucked into bed. He was filled with the wonder and dreams of the world of trains and all it might convey.

For the entire year Floyd only talked about his love of trains and he wanted a set of Lionel trains of his own. Lionel trains are exact duplicate miniatures of the real McCoy, perfect in every detail and extremely expensive.

Many years ago people made up elaborate platforms complete with tiny towns. There were stores, schools, churches and tracks which ran all through the town and around the platform. The trains had all the bells and whistles, crossroad signals and tunnels one could possibly imagine and afford.

Floyd's Daddy worked hard and by the end of Floyd's fourth year, he was very happy when Santa Claus brought him a set of Lionel trains on a small platform.

Floyd played endlessly with the trains and he knew the names of all the companies painted on each boxcar. He knew how to operate the trains making them stop and go, up and down the little hills and stopping at various stations. Floyd lived for his Lionels.

When Floyd was six his Daddy taught him to put the platform together and set up the trains. After the Christmas holidays, Floyd and Daddy took it all apart and put them away again. It was a lot of work but Floyd loved every minute, at least the setting-up part. He didn't care much for taking it all down and packing it away.

Daddy decided to set up the larger platform in their basement so that Floyd could play with his Lionels whenever he wanted. At first it seemed like a great idea.

As time wore on, Floyd began to get bored with the whole scenario. There was noone else to share in the fun and he disliked playing in the basement by himself. It just wasn't the same, he thought. Now blowing the train whistle was stupid. There wasn't anyone around to hear it but himself and the trains needed so much care. Why, they were more work than taking care of the dog. The wheels needed oiling and the lights had to be checked and the wiring had to be just so. Sometimes when Floyd ran the trains too fast, they would jump the tracks and he'd have to reassemble the entire line-up and that's when the timers needed to be reset.

Once when the trains went off-track, they slammed into the little mirror lake breaking the mirror and knocking down a whole set of trees and a couple of houses. Floyd took out a few of the other buildings to replace the damaged ones and there was no more lake and the trees looked really bad. Once in a while there would be a jam-up in the tunnel so Floyd decided to get rid of that also.

Another time when his cousin came to visit, he knocked out a few wires by stepping into them and he short-circuited the mechanism that operated the crossbars and blinkers so they didn't function properly. Now, without the lake, the bridge didn't make a whole lot of sense so Floyd decided to remove that, too.

Within a year many of the town buildings, bridges, tunnels, lakes, crossbars and trees were missing from the scenic platform that was once a little fairyland toy town. It just didn't look the same or feel the same. There were no whistle stops and blinking lights, there was no station and some of the fenceposts were destroyed or fallen.

Floyd looked at his train dream world as a disaster area. The glamour was gone; the thrill was gone. Floyd turned off the lights of his little train town and left them. He never realized that something so lovely would require so much work and time.

Santa Claus never left any instructions about taking care of a train. Floyd sat and wondered what made it always look so easy? Darned if he knew.

Do I know which house Floyd lives in? I think so. It's the one with the sign out front that reads "TRAIN FOR SALE."

* * * *

Lloyd and **Cecelia Corbellan** are from the outskirts of Detroit. Lloyd and Cecelia worked in the automobile industry for several years. They now own a card and gift shop and they sell several small toys. Sorry, no trains.

SECOND CHANCE

JESUS MENTERO

IN A SECTION OF HARLEM there were several guys' clubs with catch names. One was a particularly strong group known as The Gunners. They didn't carry guns, although that might have been partly true; but, they gunned their motorcycle engines so loudly, it rocked the entire neighborhood.

The club was made up of Irish, blacks, Italians, a few biker babes, one or two gypsies and some other league-of-nations backgrounds. They hung out at a corner tattoo parlor which probably fronted for a backroom card game and whatever other dealings came down the pike. It would have come as no surprise if a lot of cocaine went down and a minor league of deals around other drugs, some marijuana, probably some Ecstacy changed hands. No big deal.

Here is the story in Mike's own words, (unedited slang) about his son, Jesus.

"You wanted somethin' you got it. All you needed was cash. They stopped frontin' guys a long time ago when some kid named Turk got blitzed for not turnin' over the money at the right time. If you were late once, they made you pay the vig (interest) but you had to meet your deadline, or else. Turk didn't get it, so they cut off his hand and sent it home."

Now and then somebody wound up in the ER sliced six ways from Sunday or dumped in the morgue after being fished out of the river. That only happened after you got the crap kicked out of you but first, they rearranged your face a little. Just enough so nobody could recognize you, you know what I mean? Hey! Rules are rules. You play, you pay, awright?"

"Now there's this kid, some dummy from the Bronx, who wants "in", but he's a nobody. He was a pain in the a__ and nobody wanted nothin' to do with him.

His bike looks like somethin' outta the dump, he's got no great history for doin' anything big time, and what's worse, his name is Jesus (say: Hay-soos). Omigod, did that smack of trouble! He got more flack for bein' a spic than for bein' stupid.

They told him to get lost more than one time but he kept comin' back. (Tapping on his temple) Dense. He just didn't get it, y'know?

Why he wanted to get in with them, who knows? Maybe make a name for himself, y'know what I mean? Anyway, he asks around about what he had to do to get in with those guys.

They used him. They made him a gopher for every dirty job they could dream up. Once they made him rob a car. Well, that wasn't too bad 'cept it belonged to the Chief of Police. Not too swift, if you know what I mean, right?

Anyway, he was a runner collectin' money from hookers, sorta like a pimp. But, he wasn't the main guy who got all the money. Jesus just got a few beans (drugs) for doin' the dirty work. He didn't care, he just wanted to get looked at, not looked over, y'know?

Well, that went on for about a year or more and they treated him like scum. You know why? Because that's what they thought he was. But...what they didn't know was that this kid was tough. He took everything on the chin including a couple of sucker punches. A black eye here and there, a few teeth out, that's what happens if you stick your neck out too far. Hey, that's what you gotta do if you wanna make points.

Well, anyway, Jesus took just so much and no more. He just couldn't take no more. So, one day he decides he's gonna do somethin' really big and get his fifteen minutes of fame. So he offers to take on some big responsibility from the head honcho so he can maybe move up a little in the club.

He gets an appointment and he goes to see the top guy. He asks for a tough assignment so he can make a good impression, like he wants to get noticed, right? Well, the Captain is thinkin', 'What's this punk want from me? He can't take 'no' for an answer so I'm gonna give him a chance. Yeah, I'll give him a big chance and see how he makes out.' "

"So he calls in the kid and says to him, 'Listen, Jesus Christ Superstar, you wanna do somethin' big, I hear, right? Well, I'm gonna see you get your chance.' "

Next Friday night there's gonna be a very important meetin' of the heads of two clubs from the other end of Harlem and us. It's gonna be like a preliminary election to see who's gonna head these clubs up. Well, up 'til now, you know I'm the boss. They don't have the same ideas so I'm gonna have to do a little housecleaning and you're gonna help me, ok? So far I heard some things about you like you got ambitions. I like that, that's ok. But, don't get any bright ideas about climbin' the ladder overnight, see. I'm the head of this outfit and I'm stayin' here. You and nobody else is gonna' take me outta my job. Just do what you're told and everything'll be fine, ok?'"

Jesus didn't dare to speak. It was disrespectful to speak without permission. He just stood there listening. Behind him two bouncers were ready to take his head off if he so much as lifted an eyebrow. Jesus was scared for the first time but it was too late to do anything about it. He couldn't back out or he'd wind up like some other guys, maybe in a grave somewhere in the woods. He was around here too long and after almost two years, he knew too much. Sometimes what you know has to die with you. That's just they way the game is played. There's no room for sissies in the arena, only gladiators, ok?"

The Captain went on. "When I begin to end the meetin', if it went good, I'll give you a good look. If it didn't, you're gonna have this pipe bomb in your jacket and when I give you a signal, you're gonna heave the bomb right in the middle of the circle and blow them bastards to the moon!"

There was nothing to say. Jesus knew this was his true test and he couldn't fail. To do so would have meant the end of him. There was no turning back, no room for error.

He didn't like what he heard. He never really meant to kill anyone. He wanted to do some dirty jobs, sure, but murder just wasn't in his gut. His skin crawled. This was his moment of truth. He gave a slight nod in recognition and left. He knew he had to wait for his orders to come. All he had to do was carry them out.

Friday night was dark. No moon, no lights. It was hard to see anyone's face in the area behind the tattoo parlor. It was around 2 a.m. and the meeting would begin at 2:30 when everybody in the neighborhood was asleep. The cops ran their beat so they wouldn't be comin' back at that hour. It was safe.

Out of the darkness five cars with lights out assembled in the alley. Two from one end, three from the other. The Captain and his men, the other clubs and all their men formed a large circle and everyone spoke in whispers. Strangely enough, without much education, this group of men conducted their business in an orderly, professional manner. It was like something you'd see in a movie, only this was the real McCoy. No Hollywood fake crap goin' on here, no sir. This was it, baby."

The bomb was secured under Jesus's jacket, just like he was told to do. As the time drew closer, Jesus suddenly got cold feet about tossin' the bomb. He really didn't wanna kill nobody and yet he knew, if he didn't, they would kill him. He had to make a choice and he had to make it fast. He couldn't run. That wouldn't work. He couldn't scream. They'd quiet him for good. That stunk. He had to do this job. It's what he asked for, wasn't it?

The minutes were countin' down now. The Captain was lookin' at him real close.

Jesus was gonna get the signal any minute now, right? Things seemed to go ok, he thought, so why did he have to throw the pipe bomb? There was no argument, there was no challenge. What did it all mean? He didn't dare ask. Ask what? You wanna get rapped on the head? Sometimes a rap, if it's hard enough, could get you a cracked skull, y'know?"

Just as the meetin' was comin' to an end, the Captain looked at Jesus. Oh, jeez. Now what am I gonna do? thought Jesus. I gotta kill this guy or they're gonna kill me.

I can't do it. I can't do it! What the hell was I thinkin'? Am I nuts? All this, for what?

Jesus asked himself many questions as his life passed before his eyes. Within seconds the Captain and his men backed off several feet. Before the other men across from them knew what was about to happen, the Captain made his move. There it was. The signal came. The Captain winked at Jesus. Throw the bomb!

That's what it meant. Throw the bomb! Jesus froze. His hand went into his jacket and he withdrew the pipe bomb and just as he was about to toss it on the group standing opposite him, he simultaneously threw the bomb on the ground and himself on top of it.

"Can you believe it? He actually threw himself on the damn bomb!" Mike said.

The blast in Jesus' head was like nothing he'd ever heard. But...the explosion... never....came. It didn't happen. Jesus just laid there, dead. Or, at least, he thought he was dead. He didn't move a muscle. He didn't open his eyes. He imagined himself dead.

All at once ev'rybody started to laugh. From both sides, everyone was laughing so hard. Jesus didn't know what he was hearing so he didn't make a move

Next thing he knows, someone's pickin' him up, laughin' all the time. Jesus didn't know what to do. They stood him up and brushed him off. He just stood there like a jerk.

"It was a joke, you jackass. It was a joke. Congratulations, man! You finally earned your stripes."

Jesus had performed his final test of honor and fearlessness. He was now officially in the club. He was "one of them." Amid the laughing and the handshakes, Jesus was pounded on the back and they tousled his hair. Everyone went inside, had some drinks and around 3 a.m. the crowd split up.

Jesus was trembling the entire time he made his way back to his dinky room. He packed his few clothes and left. He had been given a second chance and he took it. Jesus went to live as far away as possible from the club and the people he had tried so hard to join.

Sometime life offers you a second chance. Sometime you have to take that chance before it gets away from you. Sometime you have to lay your life on the line to make a decision.

Sometime you lose. Sometime you win. Sometime you have to make a choice.

* * * *

Mike Montero is a good example of making choices. He never had much education but he knew enough to make an honest living by earning it. He lives in New Mexico with his wife, Tina. Mike and Tina own a small farm and they are happy to be out of the rat race.

SECTION EIGHT

* * * *

Random Acts of Kindness

HER CROWNING GLORY

LENORE FRIEDMAN

I DON'T KNOW what all the fuss is about, Lenore thought. All I want to do is cut off just enough so I could wear a ponytail like the other kids. Now I'm being grounded.

Ever since she could remember, Lenore had long hair. Her Dad always called it her "crowning glory" but for Lenore, it was a headache. The boys in school yanked it to tease her, the mosquitoes got caught in it and it took much too long to untangle when it was shampooed. Grammy always bragged Lenore was the third generation of natural redheads and that she should be so proud of her locks. Her mother said she could cut it when she was eighteen, but, she added, that she should then be prepared to leave the house.

Lenore's titian red hair was almost to her waist and it set off her pale green eyes so much that people always turned to stare at her. At fourteen she was turning heads.

On Tuesday morning the assembly hall was filled with boys and girls who were waiting to hear the guest speaker talk about "Locks for Life." This is an organization which takes donated hair and makes wigs for cancer patients who'd lost their hair through chemotherapy treatments.

As an act of love and charity, several girls and a few boys with shoulder-length hair offered to have their hair cut to perform a random act of kindness.

At last! Here was Lenore's perfect opportunity to cut her hair and do a good deed at the same time. How could her parents be angry with such good intention? she asked herself. Several of her friends were doing it but knowing how adamant Lenore's parents were on the subject, not a single one tried to convince her of it. It was her call.

With trembling lips and sweaty palms, Lenore slowly made her way to the front of the auditorium where three bar stools stood waiting in front of three hairdressers with sharpened shears in hands. Everyone was chattering as various girls left the stage with new, short hairdos.

Lenore's heart nearly stopped. She felt slightly heady as she made her way down the aisle. As she neared the forbidden spot, a quiet came over the twittering crowd. Could this actually be happening? Was she crazy? Was she prepared to leave her happy home forever?

Lenore was not very tall for her age. Now in the bright lights her long hair seemed to be like a flaming streak flowing down her back. She walked gingerly all the time wondering if everyone could hear her heart pounding? She was determined; there was no turning back. It was now or never. Isn't this what she'd been waiting for for years?

As she turned the front row of seats and made her way toward the center, she began to misstep, as if something were trying to stop her. She righted herself and moved ahead. Closer now. The blades of the scissors caught the overhead lights and flashed as if to beckon her toward them. She felt a strong pull on her body as if she were mesmerized. It's just a haircut, after all, she thought. But, was it just that? She second-guessed herself.

It was like a grand procession, Lenore and her hair making their way to the center of the stage as if some sacred ceremony were about to take place. The air was heavy with anticipation. It was so dramatic, one would think she were being sacrificed on an altar. The room was completely hushed as everyone watched. They wondered whether or not she would turn and run.

Lenore stood facing the stylist who had a blank look on her face. Lenore couldn't tell if the lady was happy or carrying a mean streak so bad she might cut off Lenore's hair to within an inch of her scalp. She didn't know whether or sit or faint.

In a very tiny voice, Lenore whispered, "Please give my hair to another young girl who can take care of it for me. I want to make this the happiest day in someone's life."

She sat on the stool, closed her eyes and prayed, all the while biting her tongue so as not to cry. She knew it would be over in a few minutes. Motioning to the nape of her neck, she indicated the length she wanted her hair cut.

In a few minutes the hairdresser held Lenore's tresses in her hand, tying a rubber band around the ends and holding out the crowning glory for everyone to see. A thunder of applause and whistles went up from the crowd. Lenore opened her eyes. At once her hands went to the back of her neck to feel for the hair that wasn't there. She looked out at the crowd and smiled. As she made her way back to her seat, friends and strangers came up and congratulated her. It was certainly a good hair day in her mind.

Sneaking into her room, Lenore wet her hair and wrapped it in a towel. Her mom was calling from the kitchen so Lenore went down to face her sentence.

She tried to explain what went on that day. As the realization of what she was about to announce hit home, her mother's face paled and she squinted her eyes at Lenore.

"You cut it, didn't you?" She asked in an emotionless voice that seemed to Lenore like her mother's last breath of life. Without answering, Lenore slowly removed the towel, too fearful to face her mother's gaze. Her mother turned her back and began to walk away.

She hissed, "You have broken my heart. I never had such beautiful hair like your father's family. My only pleasure was admiring your crowning glory and now you've taken that from me."

"From you?" Lenore asked, shockingly. "All you ever thought about was you. For once, why can't you think of someone else's life and what might make them happy? Think of the joy it might bring to some unfortunate girl who lost her own hair from cancer?"

Lenore didn't wait for an answer. She stormed out of the kitchen to seek solace in her own room. Meanwhile she thought of how she might wear her new hairdo the next day. Oh well, she thought, it's only hair. It'll grow back and she'll get over it.

Time heals and, like everything else, the months were kinder to Lenore than her mother. Slowly her hair grew to her shoulders and Lenore and her hair were growing up. They became a very glamourous team.

By her seventeenth birthday Lenore had developed a growth on her back. At first she didn't think much of it. However, she wouldn't wear a bathing suit because of the unsightly bulge over her left side closest to her spine.

One day the mirror told Lenore the lump was not something to be reckoned with. It had turned brownish and looked menacing. She showed it to her mother.

The radiologist had called Lenore and her parents to his hospital office and they went over the X-rays together. The lump was a lymphoma and it had to come out. It was necessary to have radiation and then it would be decided as to their next plan of action.

In the months that followed, Lenore was given a series of treatments and the cancer had been put into remission. However, she was warned that, like many patients, she would lose her hair. Lenore and her family were grateful for her progress and her mother gave Lenore a beautiful straw hat with a large wraparound band to wear.

About ten days later, someone from the clinic came by the house to see Lenore. In her hand she had a pretty box, a gift for Lenore from "Locks for Life." Lifting the hairpiece out of the tissue, Lenore gasped in amazement. Tumbling out of the wrapper was a long mane of hair, red in color to match her pale green eyes. The tag read, "Donated to Locks for Life from Lenore Friedman."

* * * *

Bela Friedman lives in New York with her husband and their dog, Maggie. She remembers her daughter, Lenore, with great pride and love.

GIVE US THIS DAY OUR DAILY BREAD

PARIS MAGNIN

THE FALLING SNOW magnified the silence as it slowly drifted down from an invisible sky. In the lamplight's glow the enormous flakes sparkled with faceted colors on the tips of each unique design. There they were: God and Mother Nature working their splendid craft to cover the earth with their freshly woven Angel's Blanket of white.

The awesome beauty in the stillness of night took Paris' breath away. He stepped gingerly as if not to disturb the sleeping earth beneath his feet as he made his way to the French bakery. It was very cold but the wind had ceased and the snow-laden branches on every tree resembled a Christmas card. It was nearly 3 a.m.

In his pocket Paris' fingers wrapped around the large white potato his mother left for him which would be his lunch around noon. Everyday Paris would place the pomme in the huge stone bread oven to bake. Forty-five minutes later, he would salivate as he anticipated its fluffy texture drenched in fresh creamery butter. Always the same lunch but never the same expectation. Everyday was like a different choice on a menu even though it was not new on his plate.

At ten years of age, Paris was happy to be an important entity to help support his little family. That his uncle permitted him to work in the little bake shop was a charity Paris' family would not otherwise enjoy. He worked a few hours before and after school and on weekends. He especially liked the holiday seasons. The bakery was very busy and there were many fancy torts and pastries to be made for the long line of customers the little shop boasted.

Nearing the bakery, Paris caught the sweet aroma of bread baking in the huge stone oven. Now and then the perfume of cinnamon filled his senses and he quickened his step toward the place which spelled warmth and love and food. Once inside the bakery Paris would inhale the scent of creamery butter and icing being spread over his favorite buns and hot biscuits. He offered up a little prayer of thanks.

Each morning Paris' uncle would give him a loaf of the fragrant crusty bread for the family's dinner table and he would drop off the loaf at home before heading to school.

Wrapped in paper, the baked potato in his pocket kept his fingers warm as he trudged through the snow drifts toward the school house. In Quebec the winters were long and Paris often wished he could grow up quickly so he would own a bike to traverse him faster and take him into the warm little school building.

This year Paris heard about a young girl with pretty brown hair who moved into their neighborhood. She was from a very poor family.She was three years younger so they didn't share any classes. Paris saw the girl in her tired-looking clothes and very worn shoes.

He had heard stories about her family's desperate need for assistance. Their father had died and life was an ongoing struggle for the mother who had to raise three children.

On his way home that morning Paris looked around to see if anyone was watching. At six-something in the morning it was not likely, so Paris discreetly placed the loaf of bread and the baked potato on the top doorstep of the little girl's house. He would miss his lunch that day but somehow it didn't matter. He experienced an inner glow as he walked homeward.

The next day Paris asked his uncle if he could have two loaves of bread as his sisters were getting bigger and the family needed a little more food. Gratefully Paris took the two loaves and the baked potato on his usual route. Stopping at the little girl's house, Paris left his baked potato and one loaf of bread on the top step and continued on his way.

This ritual went on for days and weeks and soon it turned into months. Paris was so happy to be helping a family in greater need than his own and he still had a loaf of bread for his mother's dinner table. He missed the baked potato for lunch but he managed to gather small broken rolls and misshapen loaves that couldn't be sold at any price. Now and then his uncle gave him a handful of broken cookies or a handful of raisins. Paris had no trouble parting with the potato and he felt he was being equally rewarded.

For his thirteenth birthday Paris' uncle gave him a small raise. He was bigger now and he could handle the heavy flour sacks. He learned to stoke the ovens and stack the shelves in the front of the bakery. He cleaned the equipment and learned to bake bread.

Paris never missed a morning to drop off a loaf of bread and a baked potato to the poor family on his journey home. It had been nearly three years since he gave up his baked potatoes yet he never missed them. He now had some money to buy a small sandwich at lunchtime and he knew in his heart somewhere a poor family was given help.

Some years later Paris had taken a job in another part of the city and he no longer lived at home. His college training took longer than usual because he had to work while attending classes. His sisters were married and his parents still lived in their home.

One day while driving to work, Paris' car was hit by a huge truck which had lost control on an icy roadway and pinned his car against the side of a security fence. Paris was lucky enough to survive with only a broken leg and he was hospitalized for a short time.

In the rehabilitation center Paris was learning to walk and receiving therapy for his damaged nerves. The nurses and physical therapists were nuns from a local convent. The work was hard but these nuns toiled tirelessly. No matter how difficult the task, they always managed a smile and a friendly word to everyone. Paris was very impressed.

Sister Jean-Marie was a lively take-charge person with a will of steel. Her orders came sweetly as her charming smile but she ruled with a determined hand. Her patients were not allowed to slack in their therapy regimens in spite of their persistent aches and pains. Paris liked her bossy attitude coupled with a motherly intention to do good.

It was only by coincidence that Paris learned that the hospital kitchen baked their own bread. One morning the solarium was dark and dreary from an overcast sky so Paris made his way down the hall which led to the bakery area. Stepping inside a sudden rush of nostalgia came over him as he smelled the fresh bread baking in the stone hearth oven.

Standing at a long work table was Sister Jean-Marie. She looked surprised to see Paris but she smiled and offered him a seat on the long bench. Pouring him a cup of hot coffee, Sister Jean-Marie began to speak.

She asked Paris if he believed in angels. He said that his mother had great faith in angels, that they were messengers of God. Her expression began to change as she started to unravel a story about her early years in a poor family.

She told him how every morning her mother found a loaf of fresh bread and a baked potato on their doorstep. They never knew who the angel was who helped feed their family but her mother was certain it was a direct answer to her daily prayers from the Lord.

Tears sprang to Paris' eyes and he didn't know whether or not to tell Sister Jean-Marie it was no angel bringing a miracle but a simple gesture of kindness by a young boy.

His heart swelled with joy as she continued her story. She said that her life had been fulfilled when she received her calling to join the Order of the Sisters of Charity.

Paris' loaf of bread had carried a message of hope and spiritual contentment to a family along the pathway of his life. He had helped fill an empty place with gratitude and love. It was proof that no good deed ever goes unnoticed in the eyes of the Father.

* * * *

Juliette Magnin now lives in sunny Florida and keeps in touch with Sister Jean-Marie who is now retired from the hospital for health reasons. They remember Paris with great love.

THE SANTA MENSCH

LEON MENTZ

THE MALL was replete with holiday shoppers and Salvation Army bell ringers. Holiday songs rang out on loudspeakers and monstrous ornaments hung from every rafter. Toyland was jam-packed with children waiting to sit on Santa's lap to divulge their wish lists to the most legendary elf extraordinaire.

From sidewalk coffee shops wafted the aroma of peppermint cappuccinos and fresh-baked gingerbread cookies in fancy holiday shapes and colors. People strolled in and out of stores sipping goodwill eggnogs and pumping themselves up with holiday songs and carols.

Back in the warehouse area of a popular anchor store, Leon was busy trimming Santa's gigantic sled with toys and goodies for the annual run at the local children's hospital. Every year a store executive would play Santa Claus and he would spend an entire day of the Christmas week going from one hospital to another giving out toys to children who would not make it home in time for Santa's visit.

Leon's job was very demanding and he met all his obligations responsibly. Keeping the department store's inventory required the computer skills of a mini-genius and the patience of a saint, no pun intended. Leon's religion didn't recognize saints; therefore, Saint Nicholas was for gentiles and kids under seven who still hung up their stockings every Christmas Eve.

He certainly enjoyed his own holidays but like many little children, he used to ask himself why he didn't have a Santa Claus or a Christmas tree. Didn't he like the taste of candy canes as much as other kids his age? His mom told him their sacred holidays had just as much meaning in their household and Leon should be proud of his Jewish heritage and not feel slighted. They were God's chosen people, she reminded him.

Leon was a guy people leaned on. He was always there to help. His store manager called him Mentz and because of his good nature, he was nicknamed "Mensch." Leon liked being called Mensch because his father was a well-loved man by his family and peers and he was always referred to as a "mensch," a respectable title.

Leon checked his watch. It was just after 2 p.m. Only a couple of hours to go and he could run home to dress for his girlfriend's birthday party. Tonight was the big night.

He was going to surprise her with an engagement ring. He'd been planning this for months and he knew this would be one of the most important things he'd ever done in his life. He hadn't told a soul of his intentions.

Everyone knew that he and Lauren had been an item for quite a while but Leon wasn't very assertive in matters of the heart. Or so they thought. Tonight he would prove them all wrong when he flashed that sparkler in her eyes. He wanted this to be the *piece de resistance* like you saw in the movies.

Won't his family be surprised? He thought again, Won't I be surprised?

Leon was jolted out of his reverie when his phone rang. Have you ever noticed how you almost knew when something was about to happen by the way the phone rang? Oh, come now, everyone has that intuition. There was just something about it.

On the other end his store manager's secretary informed Leon that Mr. Tyler's car was in a slight fender bender. He wouldn't be able to get down to the store to dress up in the Santa Claus costume to go out on the sled and make the hospital rounds. She said Mr. Tyler expected Leon to go in his place if he wanted to keep his job tomorrow.

Leon didn't have a minute to plead guilty when the line went dead on the other end. The store was near closing time and the last words he heard were, "Sometimes, Leon, you gotta do what you gotta do."

He was between the proverbial rock and the hard place now. Was he about to lose his job or his future wife? He would try to make Lauren understand. If she didn't, then what would it matter. On the other hand, if he had no job, he would have no Lauren anyhow. It struck him how the irony of this situation could alter his life forever and it all happened in less than a minute. He picked up the phone and dialed. Lauren's answering machine responded so Leon simply hung up. How can you explain all this in twenty seconds or less? He knew if he lost his job, asking for a written recommendation would be one step below preposterous.

Grumbling under his breath, Leon began to assemble the Santa belly to get ready for his title role in the children's hospital. He would try to call Lauren later on his cell phone. Perhaps he could call to say he broke his leg or something. Naah, that wouldn't work. Lauren knew him too well for that. Maybe he could drive his car in front of an oncoming train and go out like a hero.

Looking at the Santa belly, he thought he'd take the coward's way out. He put on the Santa belly and red coat and adjusted the beard.

Off the truck the sled was lowered onto the ground. Leon sat proudly on top with the sack of toys over his shoulder. The entrance to the hospital was anything but what he had planned for this particular December night. He dialed Lauren's number. No answer.

Upstairs in the children's ward, Leon was greeted by nurses who waved and smiled and tried to look happy. Out of various doors came the occasional whimpering cries of a small boy or girl who, for some unearthly reason, was meant to be here that night.

Leon took a deep breath and said, "Well, here goes nothing" and walked inside. Some of the children he saw were recuperating, some were in more stressful situations. He stopped to make a few Ho-Ho-Ho Santa Claus remarks and left a special toy for each child.

Making his way down the hall, he met a nurse who took his arm and said, "Santa, come with me. There's someone here who really needs to see you tonight."

Looking up from her pillow, dark eyes too large in her little face, the small girl who appeared like a doll in the large bed was a startling sight to Leon.

Above her hung an IV drip. Her tiny fingers were as pale as the linen they lay on. She seemed very tired and life seemed very pressing on her little form. Upon seeing Santa, the child let out a long sigh. It was as if she were almost running out of hope.

"Merry Christmas, honey," Leon said. He nearly choked on the words as the sight of this lovely child caused his heart to squeeze. It hurt him so deeply, he had to squint back a tear that nearly gave away his feelings.

He went on. "You didn't think Santa wouldn't be here, now did you? How could I ever forget such a pretty face? Now, what was it you wanted me to bring to you?" Leon asked reaching into his Santa sack for something he hoped might make her smile.

The nurse was standing in the semi-darkness behind him as he spoke. She said quietly, "Can you tell Santa Claus about your Christmas wish, Mollie?" Leon was glad to hear her name so he wouldn't look like a fool. Santa never forgets a name, you know. "Mollie, how could I forget that name? My sister's name is Mollie," he lied.

"Mollie, please tell me about your Christmas wish. I've got lots of goodies here for little girls like you." More fishing around in the sack. He chucked the little GI Joe and some other boys' stuff, pulling out a small wind-up puppy that yapped and wagged its tail.

"Oh, how about this, Mollie?" He put the doggie on the bed so she could see it move. Mollie shook her head 'no'. Santa is not scoring any points, Leon thought. I gotta do better than this.

"All I want is to get better so I can go home," the small voice said tearfully.

Wow! Leon thought. That's a tall order. I don't think Santa can pull that one out of his sack. He didn't know what to say. He grappled for words. Her tiny hand felt so small and weak in his own. He glanced at the clock on the wall. 10:10. He'd already been here for nearly four hours giving out gifts and talking with children. He never had a chance to call Lauren. His life was passing before his eyes but it left just as quickly. He had something far more important going on right here, right now and he was the man of the hour. Just then, nothing else was more meaningful to him than the child who laid here looking up at him, waiting for an answer. Leon leaned closer to the child. Her eyes had very dark circles, her skin was pale.

"Mollie, Santa Claus is going to do everything he can to help you get better so you can go home real soon. But first, I would like the puppy to stay here with you and keep you company. And, I want you to promise me that you will try very hard to get well so you can write to me and tell me when you are able to go home, is that a promise?"

Mollie managed a little smile. "Will you bring me some angels? My Mommy says if you call on angels to come around you, they will be there and never leave you. Please get me some angels, Santa Claus?" Mollie's hand tightened around Leon's as if she depended upon him to make her wish come true. Leon was really reaching for words here.

"Ok, Mollie. Santa Claus is going to bring you angels to stay with you and help you get better. I don't have any angels in my sack but I'll call some of them for you."

Leon didn't know what to do next. He was losing his image. In the nick of time, Leon lifted his shoulders and said, "Ok, Mollie. I'm calling the angels now. Wait and see."

Leon dialed on his cell phone and waited for a ringing. On the other end, Lauren said "Hello" and Leon cleared his throat.

"Mrs. Claus, this is Santa. I need a very special favor from you right now. I'm in the children's ward of the hospital and I'm here with Mollie who is very, very sick. She needs some angels to understand how she feels. She wants to go home for Christmas. She has asked me for a gathering of angels so she can get better. I hope you know why I'm calling because if you don't, then it won't be a good Christmas for anyone. Do you understand me?" He held his fingers crossed in his coat pocket.

Mollie's face brightened as she heard Santa Claus making a special request just for her. Mrs. Claus was now in charge of the entire situation. Mollie was beaming.

Santa went on. "I'm sorry I won't be able to get there just yet but I've had so many important visits to make at the hospital and I just had to be here for these children, right? If you could see Mollie you'd know how special she is, just like all these other kids. They needed me here more than anything else and you know Santa Claus would never let them down."

Santa hung up the phone, proud and happy that he was solving Mollie's problem, as well as his own. Mollie promised him she would sleep tonight and tomorrow she would wake up feeling better just knowing that the angels Santa Claus sent to her were there to help her through the night. Mollie's little arms reached up and gave Santa a big hug.

Santa Claus was now very sure he was doing his job in a way that would make Mrs. Claus very proud of him. He told Mollie he'd be calling her to keep checking up on her and he expected to hear only good news of her progress. She promised to do her best.

It was nearly 11 p.m. and Leon couldn't wait to get out of the Santa belly. On second thought, maybe he should just drop in at Lauren's anyhow. The lights were still on at Lauren's. He leaned on the doorbell.

The crowd had thinned out. There were only a handful of guests cleaning up and reminiscing over the party. Lauren laughed when she saw Leon in the Santa suit.

Mr. and Mrs. Mentz were shocked at first but, once Leon told them what had happened, they smiled about it said that he had done a good *mitzvah* that day. Santa Claus and Mollie had saved the day. Now Leon wondered if the angels could save Mollie. He held her in his mind and blew her a kiss from his heart.

The next day, Leon recounted the events of Santa's hospital rounds to his co-workers. They were impressed and a little surprised that Leon had taken on the Santa Claus role. Leon was feeling so good, he wore the Santa hat all day in the office.

Calling the hospital Leon learned that Mollie was showing signs of slight improvement. With continued therapy and hope from Santa Claus, she might have a good chance to make a full recovery. Leon was committed to her cause promising to check in on her periodically. He was feeling ten feet tall.

On the day of the holiday office party, Mr. Tyler handed out the Christmas checks and bonuses. On Leon's envelope were the words "To The Santa Mensch."

* * * *

Harold Mentz is a retired high school teacher who dabbles in local theater near his home in upstate New York. He also sings baritone in a barber shop quintet at the Jewish Community Center.

SECTION NINE

* * * *

Achieving The Dream

THE RAGSHOP

HELENE McNALLY

IT'S TOUGH FOR A LITTLE GIRL to grow up without her father. Helene's mother had to hold down two jobs to make ends meet. They lived in a small basement apartment and on rainy days, there was barely enough light from the little casement windows for Helene to do her homework. She despised living in a basement. A boy at school told her only rats lived in basements. It was a remark she carried with her for many years. It hurt.

Helene hardly remembered ever having a new dress. She always wore hand-me-downs from the neighbors' daughters or something her mother picked up at Salvation Army. Helene always dreamed that someday she would have a new dress from a department store.

By the time she was nine, Helene owned a large wagon with wooden side rails. On Saturdays Helene and her little friends would walk block after block of row houses collecting old newspapers and rags. When the wagon was filled up to there, they'd take the papers and rags to the local ragshop where the junkman would give them about thirty cents for every hundred pounds of newsprint.

Helene would catch him putting his finger under the scale to cheat them but she was too sharp not to notice and angrily called it to his attention. He'd scoff but finally he gave the children what money was owed them. Helene hated that he tried to swindle them out of their hard-earned cash. She vowed if she ever had a business of her own, she'd never do a single thing to cheat anyone.

It was very hard work for those boys and girls and their hands were blistered. Their little palms would bleed from pulling on the handle of that wagon, while one or two of the kids pushed the wagon from behind. They wrapped their hands with old rags and then they'd go out and do it all over again, those brave kids.

There wasn't very much small children could do to earn a little money for an ice cream cone now and then, so they were happy to work every Saturday to make pocket change. They had become a familiar sight in the neighborhood and they were happy as they went about their weekly schedule picking up bundled newsprint from cellar windows.

Every weekend Helene would empty her piggy bank to count out the money she'd earned. She only bought an ice cream cone once a month. She couldn't afford such a luxury. After all, she was putting her sweat equity into a business of her own one day.

At thirteen Helene would babysit and run errands to the local grocery store, always keeping her dream playing its familiar song in her head. Then she and her mother wouldn't have to live in a basement like rats. They would go up the steps to enter the house, not down one flight. It felt like that day might never come.

Once a boy sassed her in a sing-song voice, "Helene McNally lives in the alley." She tried to ignore the remarks and at times she swore under her breath she'd break his rotten little neck. They can think what they like but I'll show them, she thought.

When Helene was seventeen she picked up a job at a nearby clothing consignment store. With this job she could earn money and buy some better clothes at second-hand prices. She made friends with the shop's owner, Darcy, and she learned a lot about the rag business. In her spare time, Helene went to local neighbors and picked up pre-owned items of clothing. She'd repair hems, sew on loose buttons and press out the wrinkles. Darcy told her she could keep the profits from whatever clothes Helene brought in on her spare time.

The work went well for nearly two years, then Darcy lost her lease. She decided to retire, so she and Helene parted friends. Helene decided it was time to make some changes.

Never having had a vacation, Helene took some of her hard-earned money and went to London. One rainy afternoon she ducked into a little tearoom to get out of the drizzle. In a small booth by the window, she warmed her hands over a cup of hot tea. She picked up a newspaper someone had carelessly tossed aside on the seat next to her. Looking at the want ads, Helene's eyes fell upon the Business Opportunities column. A very small ad mentioned a uniform store that was going out of business with leftovers for sale at negotiable prices.

Not knowing her way around town, Helene hopped into a taxi and went to check out the ad which beckoned to her gut instincts. This is insane, she thought. Oh well, nothing ventured, nothing gained. She didn't have anything better to do that day anyhow.

The little store was in a blue-collar neighborhood with a beat-up sign and a window with a huge crack. The shop's owner was packing cartons when Helene arrived. She stopped to chat with Helene and made tea in the little two-room studio behind the store which she used for storage. Helene's heart jumped for joy over the little studio. It might be the perfect place for her to live and look after her own little business, she thought.

"Wait a minute. I came here for a vacation, not to buy a business," she exclaimed. The owner smiled and said, "Some things just happen when we're not looking for them."

Within the time it takes to sip two cups of tea, Helene and the shopkeeper struck up the deal of the century and Helene even offered to buy the showcases. The ladies got along as if they were old friends. It was dark by the time all the details were worked out.

When she was leaving the little store, Helene got a hug and a key. The owner told her she could come in over the weekend to fix up the place and she would give her ten days' free rent to the first of the month. Helene was never happier as she made frantic plans to relocate and start a new business and a new life.

The next few days were busy as Helene went out to meet and talk with the locals. She hired a handyman down the street who showed up with paint brushes and rags. Her new cell phone was a saving grace and soon she would learn to drive on the opposite side of the roadway.

Helene went to all her new neighbors and asked for pre-owned clothing to sell in her new shop. She placed a small ad in a local paper asking for donations and offering a good discount to those people during the first week of her store opening. Life was good.

She set up a tiny kitchen/living-room in the adjoining room and a second-hand rug helped turn the little back room area into a bedroom. For the first time in years Helene didn't have to walk down a flight of steps to get to her apartment. It was a great feeling.

Helene's neighbors were delighted to see an American girl in their midst who made herself a part of the neighborhood with ease and charm. The "Coming Soon" sign and her open door invited passersby to stop in and pick up her flyer of "Opening Specials." Helene was enthralled with the new "slang" she was learning and she laughed whenever she made an innocent mistake.

Night after night, when the neighborhood was asleep, Helene worked to set up her "dream workshop" as she liked to call it. Sewing, mending, ironing and pricing the clothing kept her busy. Helene had to learn a whole new way of handling pounds, ringing up her associates and getting used to new phrases to which she had no clue. Life was fun at worst.

She'd often stop and pinch herself in disbelief. Whoever would have thought that little Helene McNally who lived in the alley would become a proud shopkeeper in London?

As the opening day drew near, Helene hung an angel over the doorway to bring her good luck and good friends. She vowed her guardian angel had brought her to this place.

At last the day of the Grand Opening arrived. The most exciting time of Helene's life came when she looked at the beautiful new sign hanging out over the front window. With a wink at her angel, Helene smiled warmly as she greeted everyone who entered her store that day saying, "Welcome to the Ragshop".

* * * *

Mary McNally retired in London to be near Helene. In more recent years she came back to the United States and she keeps the little "Ragshop Angel" on the bedroom dresser. Mary likes to read and play bridge. She also likes to brag about her daughter, Helene, who took them out of the basement apartment for good.

SINGIN' MAH WAY TO HEAVEN

SUGAR CANDY

I WANNA TELL YOU A STORY 'bout my li'l girl, Sugar Candy, who left me an' her brothers an' this beautiful world at the tender age of seven by singin' her way to Heaven. But it be best if I start at the very beginnin'. Growin' up ina backwoods o' Al'bama was prob'ly one o' Life's most daring experiences. Now seein's I'm a grown woman, I see what dat meant but at dat time, the kids didn't know nothin' diff'rnt than what talk they mightta heard from dere elders.

E'ry family had aunts, uncles, cousins, old folks an' newborns usually livin' under one roof an' that weren't nothin' rare in them days. They was always too many of us and not enough o' anything else that held us back 'cept everyone lived the same so wha'dit matter.

Our li'l house was just a square hut, made outta wood my Poppa brought home. We saved it fo' a long time so we could build us a place. Him and Eli would ride into town in the wagon when the roads was dry. If dey was too wet and muddy, ol' Banjo would jes slip an' slide and his legs would go out from under him an' he couldn't pull dat wagon.

Poppa got some old metal to shut the wind out da windows an' Poppa made a real big fireplace so we could all sit 'round it in the winter. We never let the fire go out so's we wasn't gonna freeze to death. Momma got up early at the sunrise and she'd start cookin' for our dinner. We ate soups mostly made from the garden Poppa planted out back. It was the best thing we had and when Sugar went out to help Poppa, she would be singin' "Amazin' Grace" at the top o' her voice.

Well, when Momma made a big pot of soup we had goods to eat. Auntie Jean would make bread an' jellies from the wild berries that grow'd out back on a little fence. We was sure lucky to have that berry patch, I tell ya.

Poppa got us a li'l pig an' he spent all his time fattenin' it up on some corn. Lotsa times we wan'da eat dat corn but Poppa said no 'cause we hadda make dat pig fat so when da winter come, we had a pig in our smokehouse so we could fill up our bellies in the cold winter.

I remember one time when dat li'l piggy got inta Momma's li'l milk can what had some o'dat ole goat's milk an' she drank the milk and got so full, why she jes couldn't back out dat milk can. She was squealin' an' squealin' like somebody tried killin' her. We jes hadda laugh 'bout it 'cause Poppa said we would wait 'til her belly went down an' she would back out by h'self. Well, we got that pig up to size for a whole year an' when Poppa said it come time to kill it, we was all sad an' happy 'bout it 'cause den we knew we was gonna have food that winter. It was God's way, y'know, of givin' us His blessin's.

My Momma yusta sweep out our floor e'ryday sayin' she was sweepin' the devil out the house. We oney had a dirt floor so I never could figger out what she was sweepin' but thas' what her Momma tol' her so I guess it stuck as it go down da line o'family.

Well, Sugar was a happy chile 'cause she had her voice to sing an' sing she did! Poppa yusta say, "Sugar Candy, someday you gonna sing to the whole world!" an' Sugar would make up some words jes' so she could show off to Poppa an' make him happy.

My brothas was so diff'ernt, Momma said she didn't know how they come out the same place. Eli was quiet an' sweet; George was resentful an' hated his life 'cause we was po'. Poppa said we had to take care of his Momma an' Poppa 'cause they was slaves, too, an' they took care o' him an' they came out awright once they got dere freedom.

Granddaddy kept up good as he could; Granmammy was near blind so she jes' sat on the porch smokin' her old pipe most o' the day an' singin' the songs we learned as kids. They was mostly spir'chal songs handed down but the wisdom in them songs was the way everyone learned their lessons in Life. We learned from singin' to love an' praise God, do right an' work hard. Some songs told us how our ancestors got here from Africa an' some songs jes' told how they got killed for jes' bein' black. Seems to me we was better off jes' stayin' in Africa. We never aks'd to be taken out from there in the firs' place.

Poppa said we had to be real polite to the Massah 'cause they gave us this here place to live in an' some jobs on the farm so we hadda 'preciate it an' keep workin'. Well, my man an' I wasn't 'bout to complain none but we wasn't sure this was the only way to get by. We heard tell down by the railroad there was folks lookin' for young'uns to work if they had strong backs an' then some girls to keep house an' cook an' like that.

Well, my brotha George, now he didn't like takin' tough talk from them white folks an' he was workin' up at the big house on the Garrison Plantation. Well, you see, there was this young lady 'roun 'bout sixteen an' she was talkin' wit him an' he was tol' never be talkin' with the white ladies. Well, one night she went down to where he was stayin' in the stable an' she was talkin' an' he din' answer non 'cause he was so scared. She made up some story 'bout losin' her bonnet an' he hadda come wit her to go lookin' for it. He din' wanna go but she said she was gonna tell her Daddy an' he would get a beatin' so he went to help her. I always knew dat George was stupid but he rather be stupid den catch a beatin', if you know what I mean. So he jes went wit dat lady never knowing any better.

Dat lady's bonnet was blowin' in the dirt an' all wet an' muddy.Well, she tol' George to get her bonnet an' get it clean again. Well, when dey got back it was late an' her Daddy saw George wit dat lady's bonnet in his hands, he din' wait for no answers. He jes' got some men an' dey tied up George to a big tree an' dey beat him, they did. No sir, no poor black man's gotta be talkin' to no white ladies, no matter what it be about.

Since dat time, we never went anyplace near dos plantations so we din' never get no work again. I was already in the next house down the road an' I was a washer woman. I got to eat pretty nice awright but almost never come home to see Momma an' Poppa. So, to keep dat job I was Massah's mistress an' dat's how I come to have li'l Sugar Candy. Y'know, is all part o'the job, if you know what I mean. (Wink)

Well, Sugar Candy was growin' up to be a singer, I swear to God she was. Dat chile had a voice like a songbird an' she was singin' since she could talk by age three. E'ry Sunday Sugar was at the top of her voice in the church 'cause she was gonna grow up to be a star someday an' go to the big city soon's she could get out da house. Heck, there weren't nuthin' we could do to he'p her much so she was gonna be on her own anyways.

I can see her now standin' up dere. She had her little braids tied up so nice with a ribbon from a box a nice lady in the church gave to her. Why she even had a new pair o' shoes from that charity place what yusta come to the church an' be bringin' us some food rations. Once in a while my Momma even got a nice dress or a piece o' cloth to make a curtain. Sometimes Momma let me wear her dress so I could go hear Sugar sing at church.

Well, my Sugar was gonna sing in our little wooden church on that first Sunday in November. We yusta love dat time o' year 'cause the leaves would fall all 'round an' they covered the ground all red an' gold. Made it kinda look like a picture next to dat church.

Dat was when Eli went to cut the wood for the church to get it ready for the winter when we had to make a fire in the stove to keep it a bit warm lessen the snows would freeze it up.

One Friday night them kids was practicin' their hymns and we was gonna go an' get some potatoes an' make somethin' to eat when we got back. But the kids hadda stay dere rehearsin' the songs they was gonna sing dat next Sunday mornin'. Why, we could hear dat li'l church organ carry its song on the evenin' breeze as we was comin' on the road with ol' Banjo pulling Poppa's wagon. But dis night, Lord spare us, was differ'nt.

We was comin' down the road near the church when we saw the fire. It was all up in the sky an' the whole place was burnin' to the ground. They was people e'rywhere but they couldn't get nowheres near it 'cause them flames was already too much an' nobody was dere when it happened. Them chir'ens was burned in that fire an' we couldn't do a thing to save 'em. When the screamin' died down outside, we could only wait 'til the fire burned itself out 'fore anyone could even get near it. That whole place went down in flames an' my li'l Sugar was never able to sing again. (She sobbed.)

The good Lord took my Sugar an' them other li'l kids 'fore they ever got a chance to live some. My Sugar's life to be a singin' star weren't never gonna happen no more now. Dem other kids, too, their Mommas got their hearts all broken as well. Think they didn't feel the pain? Well, they musta 'cause next week we heard our neighbor lady went an' killed herself 'cause her son were all she had an' for her dere weren't nothin' left to live for so she went on to meet her Maker jes' like her boy did. Poor lady.

Well, now, all I can say here is dat my Sugar is surely on her way awright. I know she was jus' singin' her way to Heaven.

* * * *

Mrs. Rosella Candy has requested her city be withheld. She is a housekeeper in a private home, far more educated than when this story took place. She has asked us to print it just as she remembered it...and we did.

NO RITE OF PASSAGE

PHILIPPE CHENIER

IN HIS LITTLE TOWN outside of Johannesburg, Philippe lived in a hovel with his mother, Phatimah, and three younger sisters. In one room life had to make its cursed way under the African sun. Most of the babies nursing at their mother's breasts were being lied to as they prayed for death to come soon so they could all be out of their misery.

The babies were so weak they hadn't the strength in their bony arms to shoo away the hundreds of flies that swarmed on their emaciated pitiful faces. Their eyes were like huge golf balls in their thinly covered skulls. If they didn't die from starvation, surely they would have expired from the infectious sores that covered more of their tiny bodies than any clothes they might have hoped for.

Philippe turned away in sadness and disgust each time he witnessed such a scene. All he could think of was growing up and going to America where he could be free and fed. It was like some kind of a sick joke, being planted in this God-forsaken area. Better they would all burn in Hell for this was no better. His mother's futile attempts to pray was a mockery in his eyes. Here there was no God to hear them. If there were, He would have been here by now.

"How does one get so unlucky to be born in such a miserable place?" he asked himself.

Luck had nothing to do with it, he realized. They had been here for generations and this is where their seed was planted. Nothing more. It couldn't happen any other way.

His little sisters were destined for a fate worse than Philippe's. At least he was a male and he would make his way out of this place when he was a little older and taller.

Philippe tried to work loading up trucks with bundles of wood. By nighttime his arms were so weary, he didn't know which pain was greater; the pain in his arms or the hunger pain in his belly.

"Ameddicah, Ameddicah. All I want to do is get to Ameddicah," he voiced his thoughts. No originality. Everyone wants to go to Ameddicah. He could dream anyhow.

When Philippe was nearly fifteen, he told Phatimah he was leaving. He had no money, just a vision. There was no justice or reason to stop him, his mother thought. What could he do here but wait to die? He might die on the journey, what's the difference? She blessed him and waved him off. All their days were numbered.

Philippe headed north toward Morocco, stealing whatever he could find to eat, working now and then on trucks loading supplies that went from town to town and finally, hitching a ride as long as it was going north. Each mile took him closer to his dream, to Ameddicah. He would get to Ameddicah if he wound up in a pine box. What did he have to lose? Sometimes he wished someone would kill him so he wouldn't have to face another day. He swore he would find a better way or die trying.

Hitching a ride one day he saw a woman burying her newborn baby in a ditch. Her other little boy stood nearby holding his pee pee while he peed in the road. Philippe wondered why the boy would hold out his pee pee when he had no clothes to wet on. It seemed ironic but to Philippe, all of Life was ironic from where he stood.

Approaching Morocco Philippe could see a different world emerging. Here was a busy place for busy people. Open markets were reeking with the aroma of olives and the ground was slick with the rich oils they oozed. Barrels stood around filled with wonderful spices he had heard of but he'd never seen or tasted.

Here and there an occasional camel waited for its owner to backpack him and commence a trek to some fantastic destination, even if it happened to be around the corner. To Philippe the newness of this amazing place was so awesome, his mind conjured up all sorts of dreams, wild and adventurous.

He quickly made friends with a man who owned such a little open market. He was hired on the spot to help with the barrels and tend the camel. He was placed on night watch and allowed to sleep on a mat in the back of the stall. He had never seen so much food in one place and he made himself ill stuffing his belly with olives of every kind.

The owner and his wife were a middle-aged couple who liked Philippe and took pity on him. They sent him on errands and in exchange, he was given some of their food to eat. He ate bread everyday and wished he could send some food back to his mother and sisters. Someday, he thought. Someday.

Philippe put some meat on his bones right away, he felt stronger and he was able to work more hours. He learned many new words and he wished he had some schooling so he could make a real living like the middle-aged couple. They could read and write.

Philippe stayed in Morocco and he learned so much in one year, he was able to make change for the customers and now he even learned to write his own name. He was getting up in the world. They would be very proud of him when he got to Ameddicah.

Within less than three years, Philippe felt it was time to move on. He had saved a little money and now he wore sandals and underwear. He had earned his manhood. He spoke with people who told him about the boats that left the harbor for Gibraltar and he wanted to know what it felt like to actually cross the ocean. 'Someday' is coming now.

Philippe was taking packages to the docks for the stall owners and there he would pick up the money for the olives he carried. An invoice was signed and Philippe would go back for another order later in the week. He loved this new job but he never spoke with men on the docks about working on the boats. They said he needed to learn to read and write but Philippe pretended not to understand them. He had a new plan formulating.

They might give him a job loading cargo on this side and unloading it on Gibraltar. It was an open door in Philippe's eyes. Another step on his journey to Ameddicah, he thought.

After a few months he began delivering the packages to the opposite side. He'd get the invoice signed and return to Morocco with the money for the shop owners.

One day he got to the port of Gibraltar but he wouldn't hand over the packages. The guard recognized him and said, "It's okay. He has no money or papers and he has to go back to Morocco. Just leave him alone." They turned their attention away from Philippe.

Suddenly Philippe pretended to be ill and he fainted. The guards picked him up and carried him to a tiny back room in the station and put him on a small cot. They said it was "heat exhaustion" as they went back to work. Amid the hustle and bustle, no one gave much thought to Philippe. As soon as the boat pulled away from the pier, Philippe jumped onto the cot, out of the window and ran as fast as he could into the brush that led up the mountainside to the top of the Rock.

In the distance Philippe could see the boat returning to the port of Morocco and he let out a sigh of relief. It was very hot so he went to the little First Aid Station for tourists situated on top of the Rock. He got a container of water and went back to his hiding place.

He hid there and from his vantage point he could see the magnificent cruise ships in the harbor below. They looked like glamorous monsters floating on the water. He had never seen anything so wonderful and elegant. He wondered why the rich people in Ameddicah would spend their riches to come and look at a rock when they had everything their hearts could wish for right there in his beloved Ameddicah. 'Twas a puzzlement.

When the sun set, Philippe sensed a feeling of peace and contentment and finally, he drifted off to dream the usual dream about his future in Ameddicah. It was the only dream he ever had but one he never tired of. It sustained him and gave him hope.

Watching carefully from his perch, Philippe saw the tourists who flocked to the Rock to frolic with the Barbary apes and take silly pictures with their camcorders. What thrill could they derive from seeing a bunch of dirty monkeys? They were only two or three feet tall. The apes in Africa that Philippe had seen were the size of a man and not to be frolicked with. There was tonnage; here were peanut pushers, he laughed.

He didn't want to appear as a beggar for fear he'd be caught and sent away. Very unassumingly he went and sat on a curb near the tourists. Looking very forlornly at the apes who jumped and bounced around for peanuts, Philippe caught onto the game very quickly. Instantly, he began to jump up and down and pretended to reach for peanuts and the tourists laughed and took his picture over and over. When he stuffed too many peanuts into his mouth, occasionally a tourist would hand him a dollar or a Coke. The first time he swallowed it was so cold and fizzy, it went up his nose and he choked on it. When everyone laughed, Philippe laughed with them. He quickly won their admiration.

Counting out his little bit of money, Philippe bought something to eat at a tourist stand. When he pretended to be hungry and pick around the trash, the tourists would buy him a burger or two. His plan was working out very nicely for a country boy.

One day a tourist left a backpack behind. Philippe put on the t-shirt, shorts and sneakers and with the pack on his back, he made his way down to the cruise ship pier.

There was another small boat nearby which was registered in the Bahamas. Right then Philippe knew what he had to do. He offered to help load some cargo. When the coast was clear (no pun intended), he stowed himself down in the hold and covered himself with an old roll of burlap which had been used to cover olive barrels. He knew if he were caught, he'd either go to jail or be sent back to Africa. At least in jail he would be fed. In Africa he would be killed for various minor reasons. He prayed for the jail sentence and that the little boat would weigh anchor and head for the Bahamas, one step closer to his beloved destination — Ameddicah. In the middle of his prayer, he slept.

The next morning dawned early and Philippe awoke to the rocking of the boat. He nearly cried with joy at the thought that he had successfully stowed away and no one had discovered him. At least, not yet. And, if they did, would he be tossed in the ocean to drown? He had to leave the answer up to a lesser god; the better One would surely look after him.

When finally he was found out, he was starving and cramped beyond belief. The sailors were Bahamian so they welcomed him. They fed him. Once they gave him a huge hot pepper with meat in a sandwich. He took a big bite and swallowed. His mouth was suddenly on fire and his eyes began to water. He gasped for breath and broke out in a sweat. He could hardly breathe. The sailors roared with laughter.

Philippe thought this was his punishment for his misdeeds and that he was going to die as penance. He wheezed as he tried frantically to catch his breath. He let out a painful moan as his throat felt like it was in flames.

Amid the uproar and yells of the sailors, Philippe grabbed desperately at a bottle of water which sat on the table nearby. Philippe downed a slosh of water pouring it into his mouth and onto his face. More laughing. They played with him and they became friends, slapping him on the back and laughing some more. He had officially been "initiated" into the family, they said.

The sailors told Philippe they were breaking the rules by keeping a stowaway and told him they would drop him off in the Bahamas rather than feed him to the sharks. Since Philippe had no legal papers, they were also taking a chance harboring a fugitive.

He may have to jump overboard and swim in when they neared the shore but Philippe wasn't worried about that very much. He would probably catch a fishing boat nearby and make his way inland. God's plan was set in place and Philippe was determined to let it happen. His time for good luck had finally come.

In the Bahamas Philippe was amazed at the progressive life going on around him. He got a job on a fishing vessel and he had plenty to eat now. Life was worth living for the first time since his creation. He would work his fingers to the bone to earn his passage so one day he would be able to go to Ameddicah. Imagine, Philippe in Ameddicah. Every so often he would think of it and he'd laugh out loud.

Once he got enough money saved, Philippe went to school in his spare time. In a reasonable period of time, he got his papers with the help of a sponsor. Working harder than ever, he managed to send money for Phatimah to come to the Bahamas where she found work as a housekeeper. There she had free room and board and a weekly stipend.

By the time Philippe was twenty-two, he had a decent job and a place to live. The only thing now on his side was his dream. His ever present dream of Ameddicah.

The work was hard but Philippe was happy. He was strong and there would be time for easier work when he got to Ameddicah. He would read and write and work like any other person. Maybe someday he would learn to use a computer like everyone else.

One day a nagging pain in his stomach told Philippe it was time to see a doctor. He had never been to a hospital before and the free food was like a miracle from Heaven. He had a clean bed, three meals a day and all the care God's children could ever hope for. Who said being sick was such a terrible thing? He was not in Africa, after all.

The pain had gotten much worse now and he wondered how long he would have to stay in the hospital after the operation. He wished it could be for a long time because he had a television set and air-conditioning and all the comforts of a home in Ameddicah.

The appendix had ruptured and Philippe had been too slow getting help. They had to operate immediately. As he was wheeled into the operating room, Philippe closed his eyes and dreamed of his beloved Ameddicah. Maybe soon he might be going....

* * * *

Phatimah Chenier remained in the Bahamas and works as a live-in housekeeper. After the following two years she stood at the rail of a small cruise ship and watched the sunrise as they drew closer to the Port of Miami. When she stepped off the gangway, she knelt down and kissing her fingers, she touched the ground of Ameddicah out of love for her dear son, Philippe. With tears in her eyes, she said, "Philippe, this trip is for you."

HERE COMES THE MUMMERS PARADE

KATHY O'LEARY

KATHY O'LEARY LIVED in the City of Brotherly Lovc. The two things she loved most in her teenage years were her friends in South Philly and the String Bands of the New Year's Day Mummers Parade. Her only regret was that girls were not allowed to be a part of any Mummers String Band. Nothing personal, just an old tradition from the start.

Picture it. From their home in South Philadelphia all the way up Broad Street to City Hall and the statue of William Penn, the world-famous Mummers String Bands would march to the music they were so famous for. Dressed in their elaborate costumes and sporting baton twirlers, funny clowns and a plethora of breathtaking headdresses, these talented musicians would compete for prizes in costume originality, fancy drills and a toe-tapping, hand-clapping selection of songs to make your heart feel joyous and light.

With feathered headpieces in colors such as sparkling burgundy, lemon ice, mango slush, apricot ginger, seafoam green, robin's egg blue, luscious plum and strawberry jam, these crowd-pleasers looked like sugar-crusted rainbow cookies that were a blast to behold. Resplendent in sequins, beads and feathers, "puttin' on the ritz" was an understatement.

On many New Year Days that boasted sub-zero temperatures, the staunch people of Philadelphia layered their clothing until they almost waddled like penguins. Packing thermos bottles with hot coffee and toting woolen blankets, earmuffs and mittens, they braved the frostbiting cold with cherry-tipped noses and numb fingers and toes to hear, see and cheer their beloved String Bands. Only a blizzard could postpone this momentous event.

Vendors sold peach baskets so the crowd in the back rows could see the parade. Your Daddy's broad shoulders made a comfy perch for little toddlers head-and-shoulders above the cheering crowd. Confetti and colorful streamers flew from office windows, banners waved, shouts went up from the crowds as the Mummers strutted and danced up and down to the familiar strains of "Oh, Them Golden Slippers" and "Beer Barrel Polka."

The parade passed famous places so dear to Kathy's heart such as the Academy of Music where the late, famous Eugene Ormandy directed the Philadelphia Orchestra. Out of the halls of Philadelphia came beloved singers as Mario Lanza, Marian Anderson, Nelson Eddy (former newspaperman) and Eddie Fisher and popular singers Fabian, Frankie Avalon, Chubby Checker and Bill Haley. Famous movie stars included Sylvester

"Rocky" Stallone, Joey Bishop and comedian/actors Bill Cosby, W.C. Fields and Dom Irrera to name a few. Its ancestors included George Washington, Benjamin Franklin and William Penn. Kathy's city certainly made its mark in history.

Kathy's friends from South Philadelphia High School liked to go dancing at Wagner's Ballroom They'd board the subway at Broad Street and Snyder Avenue where many of them found the boy or girl of their dreams whose legacies are the "new kids on the block" today.

The man of Kathy's dream was a first-generation Italian who waltzed her around the floor 'til the George Summers Band closed with "I'll See You In My Dreams." Joey played a saxophone in a Mummers String Band which drew Kathy to his side. When he called her the next night and the next for a date, Kathy did little to resist.

They went roller skating and stopped at the local soda fountain to share a banana split. Movies, picnics and walks in the park on Sundays brought hugs and kisses. Joey called Kathy his Queen and promised to put a ring on her finger and a crown on her head.

They were married and had a little son name Mikey who strummed a toy banjo Daddy bought for him. Mikey played right along with his Dad and Kathy's dream was for her little son to play in the Mummers Parade String Band just like his Daddy.

When Mikey was sixteen, he was accepted as a band member and he played with his Dad who was filled with pride over his son's accomplishments. The biggest thrill came when Kathy was at band headquarters. The sensational news broke that the band had come in first place and they were awarded thousands of dollars for first prize.

Kathy was bursting with pride as she told everyone the great news, especially since Joey and Mikey were participants in the band's exciting recognition.

Now the Queen had a King and a Prince so her little royal family in the Mummers String Band was complete. Life was perfect for Kathy O'Leary.

* * * *

Theresa O'Leary never misses a New Year's Mummer's String Band Parade and the chance to see and hear her son-in-law, Joey and her grandson, Mikey. She still lives in the City of Brotherly Love and she was very happy to share Kathy's story with us.

BUSINESS IN A BRIEFCASE

JOSEPH T. BRONISZEWSKI

HAVE YOU EVER noticed how some people are just cut out to be businessmen?

There's something magical about the familiar sound of "ching-ching" to the ears of those who love making money. Mr. Joseph Thomas Broniszewski II was such a young man.

Almost from the time Joey learned the monetary difference between dimes and dollars, he had all the earmarks of an ambitious money machine. He'd make up little flyers to announce his self-promoting business. Part of it read, "If there's a small job to be done, Joey's the one to call."

The neighbors were familiar with the self-propelled fireball who would rake leaves, walk the dogs, help with household chores and take out the trash can. He might have been another Alex Keaten revisited. And all because he loved the music of a cash register.

Joey carried a well-guarded briefcase out of which he ran his "business." If you were to ask him for change of five dollars, Joey would retreat with his trusty briefcase and within minutes, you'd hear things moving, keys turning and snap locks opening. Into the room Joey would strut, head held high, chest out, broad smile, ready to do business.

Joey Broniszewski was destined for childhood greatness. At thirteen Joey bought a scooter-turned-quad with money earned from two long, hot summers mowing lawns. When he gashed his leg on the quad and required thirty-seven stitches to patch it up, he knew it was time to turn his attention to bigger things.

By the time he was a junior in high school, he earned his own shiny, red Honda Civic — a testament to hard work and a love of cash register music. Ching-ching!

* * * *

Joe, Sr. and **Janna Broniszewski** live in Philadephia, Pennsylvania with their children, Jimmy and Jenna. They enjoy summer camping, boating and going to the seashore.

LOOSE CHANGE

SISTER FRANCIS XAVIER

IT IS SAID the three greatest virtues are Love, Faith and Charity, but the greatest of these is Love. There can be no Love or Faith if there is not Charity.

In a small town in the deep south, a young Sister in a religious order chose to take a vow of poverty. She felt she wanted to give all she could to the Lord through teaching the gift of a charitable heart.

She chose to work in a tiny church whose congregation was made up primarily of poor people. They had very little money to spare yet their hearts were brimming with acts of kindness for their brethren.

Sister Francis Xavier's greatest struggle was not dealing with poverty. It was having too much money. The more she gave away, the more the church received.

Behind the small church Sister Francis planted a little vegetable garden. Back in the days of World War II people had Victory gardens to help the economy. She had tomatoes, lettuce, beets, pumpkins and all sorts of green condiments such as parsley, basil, thyme, mint and rosemary. There was also a strawberry patch for the sweet tooth.

The treasures that came from the Victory garden were immeasurable. Her convent Sisters admired Sister Francis' ambition and tenacity with her little garden and the limited funds the little church had to work with. Despite the small stipend they received from the outpourings of the parishioners, there managed to be adequate food for the winter months.

One Sunday after the service ended, an elderly woman came to ask if there were some way to help pay her mortgage as the bank was threatening to take her house in foreclosure. She had nowhere else to go and no pension as she was not able to work. Sister Francis asked everyone to sing praises to God that He would shower them with his blessings of abundance so they could help this poor elderly soul.

The next week at service Sister Francis asked everyone to please give whatever coins they had in their purses and pockets toward a collection to help the desperate old lady.

By the time the money was counted, there was a total of $217.33 which more than covered the mortgage payment. It was as if the Lord answered the prayer in the wink of an eye. The church members lifted up their voices in songs of praise and thanksgiving.

The following week, Sister Francis thanked the congregation profusely. She pointed out the church would take a collection of loose coins every week to help someone in dire need. Every week some crisis situation was met by the simple donations of loose change from the pockets and purses of the crowd. Every week, more and more money was available for desperate causes along with the regular collection monies to help pay the little bills for the church to exist upon. Every Sunday Sister Francis would turn the money over to the neediest person.

Every Sunday some poor soul's tears of sadness turned into tears of joyfulness and thanks. Every Sunday the parishioners were beaming as they dug into their pockets for their loose change.

Somehow the little charity fund grew and grew. Sister Francis turned money over to more and more needy people for food, delinquent bill payments, health care and more.

Word traveled and, within a few months, people began to pour into the little church every Sunday to offer their loose change to others in need.

Sister Francis was amazed at the miracles that were taking place every Sunday. The church that once had many empty benches was now overflowing with people, prayers and passion.

Sister Francis had a new idea. In the Springtime she invited her parishioners to plant their own victory gardens and to bring the surplus food to the church to be given out to needy families who were struggling. Within less than two months, Sister Francis had to set up a stand beside the church to put all the fruits, vegetables and staples that came in. No money ever changed hands except for the loose change collected every Sunday for the poor. The little garden behind the church had grown. Hearty men came to help till the little garden. They weeded and fertilized the plants that grew abundantly because of their belief in the act of charity.

Sister Francis asked the men of the parish if they would be willing to help build an annex to the little church so they could welcome people from surrounding areas. Very soon, the little church grew larger, the victory garden grew larger, their voices and songs of praise grew larger.

One day a huge wagon pulled up at the church. Two men carried in a small church organ which was paid for with the weekly collection of loose change. That Sunday the voices of Sister Francis' little church could be heard ringing through the trees as everyone thanked God for his goodness.

Sister Francis told everyone that the God who sent the church organ to them was the God who was living inside their hearts. It was they who made the organ possible.

It was their charity, not God's, that nurtured the abundance they all were enjoying. It was their generous spirit and their little bits of loose change that created spectacular miracles.

There was no lock on the little church door. There was only a wooden box on a stand with a little sign on it that read quite simply "Loose Change."

* * * *

Sister Francis Xavier's mother has given this story so we all may do great things for others with our own loose change. It may not be much but no man lost what he never had.

You Are Invited

* * * *

EVERY ANGEL PARENT is invited to write a story about their beloved child to share with other Angel Parents who struggle with the mystery and anguish of loss. Unlock the favorite memories in your heart and put pen to paper. Once written, you no longer have to internalize and process their departure. Sons and daughters' photo needn't remain sealed in albums and placed in a drawers separating them from you. Open a page and there they are, smiling back at us.

These pages hold the excellent moments to be cherished and preserved in the light of day. Here is your opportunity to speak easily and freely of your child while the once-empty place in your heart is filled with peace and serenity.

Our desire is to bring these wonderful memories to everyone and to help new Angel Parents who have made this transition, live the life they were intended with courage and divine spirituality.

— **Carmen D'Amico**

To submit a story:
Prepare 8.5 x 11 typed pages, doubled spaced
Include a non-returnable favorite photo of your child at any age
and send to the address below
Angel Parent
PO Box 11346
Ft. Lauderdale, FL 33339-11346

Visit us at ***www.angelparent.com***

ORDER INFORMATION

Pins: Angel Parent	$18.95
Book: ***Angel Parent Memories***	$14.95
Cassette Tapes: ***Angel Parent Memories***	$11.95
CD: ***Angel Parent Memories***	$11.95
Book & Cassette Combo: ***Angel Parent Memories***	$21.95
Book & CD Combo: ***Angel Parent Memories***	$21.95

Shipping & Handling: $2.95 each, add $2.00 for each additional order

Send Check or Money Order to
Angel Parent
PO Box 11346
Ft. Lauderdale, FL 33339-11346

To order online: www.angelparent.com